Love and Marriage
in Late Medieval London

Documents of Practice Series

General Editor

Joel Rosenthal
State University of New York at Stony Brook

Love and Marriage
in Late Medieval London

Selected, Translated, and
Introduced by

Shannon McSheffrey

Published for TEAMS
(The Consortium for the Teaching of the Middle Ages)

by

Medieval Institute Publications

WESTERN MICHIGAN UNIVERSITY

Kalamazoo, Michigan — 1995

© 1995 by the Board of the Medieval Institute

Printed in the United States of America

Typesetting by Juleen Audrey Eichinger

Cover design by Linda K. Judy

ISBN 1-879288-53-2 (pbk)

Second printing 1997

Library of Congress Cataloging-in-Publication Data

Love and marriage in late medieval London / selected, translated, and
   introduced by Shannon McSheffrey.
       p.   cm. -- (Documents of practice series)
     Includes translations from the Latin.
     Includes bibliographical references.
     ISBN 1-879288-53-2 (pbk)
     1. Marriage law--England--London--History--Sources.
     2. Matrimonial actions--England--London--History--Sources.
     3. Marriage customs and rites, Medieval--History--Sources.
     I. McSheffrey, Shannon. II. Series.
     KD753.L68   1995
     346.421'2016--dc20
     [344.2120616]   94-47339
                                                                 CIP

Contents

Acknowledgements

The following people assisted me in various ways in the preparation of this booklet: the staff at the Guildhall Library and the Greater London Record Office, Eric Carlson, Laura Gowing, Jacqueline Murray, Larry Poos, Eric Reiter, Joel Rosenthal, Bob Tittler, and the students in the 1994 class of "History of Marriage and the Family" at Concordia University. The Social Sciences and Humanities Research Council of Canada and the Faculty Development Research Fund of Concordia University both provided financial help that made this project possible. I am grateful to them all for their help.

Translations from London, Guildhall Library, MS 9065 appear by permission of the Bishop of London and the Guildhall Library, Corporation of London; translations from London, Greater London Record Office, MS DL/C/205 appear by permission of the Greater London Record Office, Corporation of London.

Introduction

The marriage tie was the foundation of social relationships in the Middle Ages. At the same time marriage formed an intimate relationship between two individuals and yet constituted a matter for public concern subject to both secular and ecclesiastical regulation. The married couple, center of the household, was the basic political and economic unit in late medieval English society. Marriage was also a religious union, a Catholic sacrament and a symbol of God's relationship with his Church. The creation of such a crucial social and religious tie was too important to be left to the man and woman on their own. God made marriage, according to the fourteenth-century English poet William Langland and his contemporaries, with the help of many people besides the two spouses:

> And thus was marriage made with an inter-
> mediate person's help
> First by the father's will and the friends' counsel,
> And then by their own assent as they two might agree.
> And in this way wedlock was wrought, and it was God
> who made it.[1]

Late medieval English people traveled the road to matrimony not on their own but in the company of family, friends, employers, and local clergy.

This pamphlet presents translations from a little-used source that sheds light on the nature of late medieval matrimony. Depositions (or testimony) in marriage cases brought before fifteenth-century English church courts reveal the attitudes and feelings of medieval people towards the marital

1

bond. They illuminate such issues as the factors considered by a man and woman in making a marriage choice, the participation and influence of family members and others in pre-nuptial negotiations, and gender differences in parts played in the initiation and maintenance of the marriage tie. As disputes about marriage were one of the most common reasons ordinary people used the ecclesiastical court system, depositions also elucidate popular attitudes towards law and the Church.

The depositions presented here come from two courts, the Consistory Court of London between 1467 and 1476 and the Commissary Court of London between 1489 and 1497. Although the vast majority of medieval records focus on the elite of society, the aristocracy and the clergy, the litigants and deponents in these cases come from lower social levels, mostly from the middling and lower ranks of the urban world. The two London courts heard cases arising from the diocese of London, which included the City and the counties of Essex and Middlesex and parts of Hertfordshire.

Most of the depositions translated here come from the City of London itself. London was the largest urban settlement in the British Isles during the Middle Ages with a fifteenth-century population of between 40,000 and 60,000 inhabitants. By modern standards this is small, and even in the Middle Ages it did not rival Continental urban centers such as Paris, which had closer to 200,000 people. London was, however, a bustling medieval metropolis and the commercial center of England, attracting immigrants from all over England and even further afield.

The depositions in marital cases offer us a view into everyday life in this medieval city: we see Londoners working and socializing, eating meals in their homes, and having

Introduction

celebratory drinks in the tavern. Many of London's inhabitants were young immigrants, who came to the city as adolescents to apprentice to a trade or to enter into domestic service. By the end of their terms as apprentices or servants, which lasted from mid-teens to mid-twenties, young men and women had often found a spouse. But young people were not the only ones who courted and married; those left bereft by the death of a husband or wife often started the whole process again after a mourning period.

Deposition evidence offers us not a complete story with a sense of closure, such as we usually get in fiction, but a vignette, an episode or two in the life of a medieval person. Scribes recorded the testimony in a case and the court's decision in separate books, and we no longer have both halves of the puzzle. One of the most frustrating aspects of this for the modern reader is the open-ended nature of the cases—we have no way of knowing how they were resolved or if the principals lived happily ever after, together or apart. The detail with which the vignettes are drawn, however, more than compensates for the lack of resolution. Some historians have, nonetheless, doubted the value of deposition evidence for the history of marriage since all marriages involved in litigation were, in some way, failed relationships and, thus, atypical. But deponents, who most frequently testified in favor of a valid marriage, were at pains to portray the process they witnessed as typical and normal. The testimony thus provides a wealth of evidence regarding what witnesses thought should be the ordinary course of events as well as the less typical reasons why marriages failed. Careful use of these depositions can provide us with a rare opportunity—one not to be missed—to examine intimate relationships between late medieval people.

3

Introduction

Church Courts and the Canon Law of Marriage

In the course of the Middle Ages, marriage came to be accepted as one of the sacraments of the Roman Catholic Church. As such, disputes about it came under the jurisdiction of church law (known as canon law) as administered through the church courts. But the Church's authority over marriage was not straightforward, because, although marriage was a sacrament, it was performed not by a priest but, rather, by the individuals who were marrying. The theology of marriage had developed in such a way that it was the exchange of *consent* of the two individuals that made the marriage bond, whatever parents, lords, or even priests might say about it. This exchange of consent was called a contract.

In the late Middle Ages, a canonically valid marriage contract was created by the exchange of present consent (that is, in verbs of the present tense) by the two principals: "I take you, X, to be my wedded wife"; "I take you, Y, to be my wedded husband." A valid marriage could also be made by future consent, the exchange of consent in the future tense—"I *will* take you . . ."—followed by consummation (i.e., sexual intercourse). An unconsummated marriage contract made by future consent (what we might call a betrothal or engagement) could be broken up by mutual consent or if one partner made a present-tense contract with someone else.

Neither exchange of present nor future consent required a priest's attendance, although the Church, of course, thought it desirable. Parties who failed to solemnize their marriage before a priest committed a sin, although they were still married. Witnesses were also not technically necessary, but the exchange of consent could not be proven without them. And no marriage could be made *without* the consent of both principals: theoretically no one could be forced into a marriage that he or she did not want.

There were technicalities, or impediments as the Church called them, which could prevent a couple from being able to marry and which automatically rendered an exchange of consent invalid. These included the impediments of consanguinity and affinity, or relationship by blood and by marriage respectively. Those too closely related to one another in either manner could not marry. In the late Middle Ages, blood relationships were considered too close if they were within the fourth degree, that is, third cousin and closer; relatives by marriage were also deemed too close within the fourth degree, so that the spouses of third cousins were also forbidden. Other impediments included impotence (usually defined as the man's inability to have sexual relations) and coercion (consent not freely given because of fear).

But dissolutions of marriage came up relatively rarely in suits brought before fifteenth-century ecclesiastical courts. Unlike modern marital litigation, the great majority of medieval cases brought to court concerned enforcement rather than dissolution of marriage contracts. The issue at stake was almost always whether or not consent had been properly exchanged and a contract made. In other words, the party bringing the suit usually wanted the court to validate the marriage, not to dissolve it.

Nonetheless, marriages did not last forever, and in some cases the courts could help bring about their demise. A marriage could end in three legally recognized ways. The first and most common way was by the death of one of the spouses; the surviving widow or widower could, and often did, marry again. Two other sorts of marriage dissolution were also available in the Middle Ages, both called divorce. We should not, however, confuse medieval divorce with the modern use of the term, as it did not refer to dissolution of a valid marriage leaving both spouses free to remarry, as it does today.

Divorce *a mensa et thoro* (literally "from table and bed") resulted in what we would call a separation. The marriage still existed, and, thus, neither party could remarry, but the spouses were no longer required to live or sleep together. By medieval canon law and theology, married people owed the "conjugal debt" or "marital debt" to one another: that is, wives or husbands could not refuse to have sexual intercourse with their spouses when asked. A divorce *a mensa et thoro* ended this obligation and the obligation to live together. This sort of suit was fairly rare; several were brought to the two courts studied here on the grounds of cruelty (see, for instance, case no. 20) and one on the grounds of adultery.

Divorce *a vinculo* ("from the bond") corresponds to what we would now call an annulment: this was granted in cases where the marital contract was invalid from the beginning and, thus, never really existed. The most common basis for a divorce *a vinculo* was prior contract or bigamy: X was already married to Y when he made a contract with Z, and thus X's marriage to Z never existed, as X could not be married to two people at once. Even so, most cases of bigamy were pursued by the original spouse trying to restore the first marriage contract rather than by the second spouse attempting to dissolve the subsequent union (see case nos. 15, 16, and 17). The impediment of coercion was cited in two cases translated below; in the first a woman claimed she had been kidnapped and forced to marry, and in the second a man alleged the woman's father physically threatened him (case nos. 18 and 19). Although some scholars have viewed the impediments of consanguinity or affinity as a common and easy escape for those who wanted to rid themselves of a wife or husband, few cases were brought on these grounds in the late medieval church courts and none in the hundreds of cases recorded in the two deposition books examined here. Divorce in the modern sense—breaking of a valid contract of marriage so that both parties may marry again—did not exist in the Middle Ages.

Why were so many people anxious to maintain contracts of marriage rather than break them up? We will never know the full answer, but several factors clearly contributed to a different attitude towards marriage dissolution and the courts. Perhaps the fundamental reason why suits brought before ecclesiastical courts were suits to enforce rather than dissolve marital contracts is that there was little point in bringing a suit to end a marriage (validly contracted) to a court that had no jurisdiction to grant a dissolution. Medieval people used the courts to their individual advantage, but their use of the court was limited by its powers and jurisdiction.

Factors external to the court system were also important. Due to high mortality rates, most medieval marriages had a relatively short span—the average fifteenth-century marriage might have lasted only fifteen to twenty years before death parted one spouse from the other. Some marriages did, of course, last forty years and even more, but disease, childbirth, and violence claimed many medieval people while they were still relatively young. In addition, medieval people probably often practiced self-divorce: unworkable marriages could be dissolved fairly easily, albeit illegally, by simple desertion. Unhappy husbands and wives could move to another part of the country where they and their marital history were unknown and they could marry again in their new place of residence. The records of the ecclesiastical courts show this happened with some frequency, although not always with success—those brought to the court had been found out (see case no. 17). But many undoubtedly succeeded and were never detected.

Suits to enforce marriages were more likely to be initiated by men than by women—the proportion in the cases translated here, men instigating two-thirds, women one-third, is approximately representative of fifteenth- and sixteenth-century patterns, with some regional and temporal variations. Because on the surface we tend to assume that marriage was more advantageous for women, especially in an economic sense, historians have had some difficulty explaining this phenomenon. Perhaps we need to re-evaluate what marriage meant both to men and to women. A spouse may have been as necessary for men as for women—the practice of men's trades was predicated on a household system and, especially, the work and support provided by a wife. We also must consider that men may have had greater access to litigation than women. Bringing a suit was expensive, and men simply had more money than women. Men were probably also more familiar with the legal workings of both ecclesiastical and secular courts because their occupations and their participation in political life were more likely to bring them into these spheres. Even behind some of the cases brought by women are signs that the woman's case was sponsored by older and politically experienced men (e.g., case no. 12).

The Laity and Marriage Litigation in Fifteenth-Century England

Medieval theology and canon law had created a system in which marriage was a sacrament and was under ecclesiastical jurisdiction. A marriage needed nothing else beyond the exchange of consent to be valid: it did not have to take place in a church or even in the presence of a priest. Indeed, depositions in fifteenth-century English courts indicate that couples often first exchanged vows of present consent without any clerical involvement. Men and women frequently married one another before witnesses in a domestic setting, through a ritualized ceremony similar to the official church rite. These marriages, known technically as private or clandestine, made up the majority of marriages brought before the church courts. The apparent typicality of private marriages according to court records may simply be due to their greater likelihood to present problems and, thus, be brought before the court. Nevertheless, the court documents portray such marriages as normal and familiar both to deponents and the court; only when they broke down did they depart from a conventional pattern. Some historians have contended that such marriages, whether they were common or rare, are evidence for the late medieval laity's attempts to circumvent the influence and participation of the Church in their lives. Others have argued, in contrast, that private marriages were probably performed not to escape ecclesiastical involvement but, rather, as a prelude to solemnization of the marriage in a church (see case no. 8). While a *marriage* was irrevocably created in the single moment in which a couple said, "I take you as my wife," and "I take you as my husband," a fifteenth-century *wedding* was not a single event but a process. After the exchange of vows in a home, "the public voice," as the depositions say, often held the couple to be husband and wife, although they would often not cohabit until after a later church solemnization.

A fifteenth-century wedding can be seen as a series of

ever-widening circles of publicity about the marriage. First, in some cases at least, the couple might exchange consent alone without witnesses (allusion is made to this in case no. 13)—although even this stage commonly involved the participation of several other parties as intermediaries (for instance, case no. 1). Second, consent was exchanged again in a domestic setting, in front of intimates: friends, family, or employers (see case nos. 1, 2, 4, 8, etc.). Third, the word about the marriage was spread through the neighborhood and parish through "public voice and fame" (see especially case nos. 11 and 13). Fourth, banns, announcements of impending solemnization, were issued in the parish church or churches of the couple, allowing anyone aware of an impediment, such as a prior marriage, to come forward (as they did in case no. 9). And fifth, the couple's marriage was solemnized by a priest in a church, either at the church door or in the nave, or body, of the church, and a nuptial mass was celebrated (see case nos. 6 and 7). This was often followed by a wedding breakfast or feast. Not all marriages followed all these stages—some, for instance, were never solemnized in a church—but many followed approximately this pattern.

The witnessing of a marriage was critical, both in a legal and a social sense. The identity of deponents—mostly men of advanced age—indicates that older male witnesses were seen as more authoritative in court than either women or younger men. The absence of female deponents in court is particularly marked for rural cases in comparison to those involving Londoners, probably indicating that difficulties of travel for women, as well as authoritativeness, were at issue. But depositions show that, in general, the principals originally asked more men to witness contracts than women; it seems clear that they saw men's presence as somehow more important.

Introduction

The social status of plaintiffs and deponents is not clearly quantifiable. The elite are not represented as plaintiffs—people of high station tended not to take such matters to church courts but instead dealt directly with the bishop of their diocese. Occasionally a "gentleman," usually not of particularly high degree, came forward as a witness (as in case no. 15). The very poor were also absent, since marital litigation was expensive. They also rarely appeared as witnesses: the indigent were deemed suspect and untrustworthy as deponents, since their poverty made them more susceptible to bribery. Deponents and plaintiffs were drawn for the most part from the middling sort: artisans, servants, and, occasionally, merchants. Even so, the cost of bringing a suit was prohibitive enough—as high as fifty shillings or more in some recorded cases—that it is unclear how servants, for instance, were able to finance it. But as Richard Helmholz has remarked, medieval people were astonishingly willing to spend large amounts of money in litigation, much like their modern counterparts.

The interaction of the canon law and popular customs regarding marriage is not as simple as the Church's imposition of its ideas on a passive and obedient laity. Laypeople had considerable knowledge of the canon law of marriage and could use it to their advantage. When they wanted a contract of marriage to be binding they adhered to canonical form as closely as they could, and when they were unsure, they prevaricated and used wording that would not commit them (see case nos. 16 and 21). The interests of the different parties in marriage did not always agree, and it was because of such conflicts that many cases were brought to court. The laity in fifteenth-century courts rarely explicitly challenged the Church's definition of what made a valid marriage or the

11

Introduction

Church's jurisdiction in marital affairs, but individuals attempted, as far as possible, to work within the established marriage system to their own benefit.

Marriage contracts were sometimes made with an eye towards future litigation (perhaps indicated in case no. 5). The testimony of witnesses indicates that steps were commonly taken by the principals, but perhaps even more commonly by witnesses, to ensure that everything in an exchange of consent went according to proper legal procedure. This could help to avoid future challenges to the contract or to ensure that any suits to enforce it would be won.

The exact words spoken in a contract were especially important. Because of this, the formal exchange of consent in a private home was often arranged and directed by a senior man, who knew the proper rituals and the correct words to ensure a valid, canonically correct marriage. This man, a sort of master of ceremonies (the name they are given in the documents is *mediator*, or intermediary), instructed the couple on the proper wording, just as a priest did in a church solemnization (see case nos. 1 and 2). Some of the depositions show popular ideas—and disagreements—about what the correct words were.

There was also a common concern that contracts be properly witnessed and sufficiently well-known. Before a formal exchange of consent in a domestic setting, the prospective spouses often asked friends, relatives, and acquaintances to come to the house to "hear what they would say to one another" (see case no. 15). Precisely because marriages could be so easily and informally made, and yet could not be unmade, it was socially imperative to disseminate widely public knowledge of a marriage. Marriages were not officially registered and recorded in England until the 1540s, so less

Introduction

official social mechanisms stepped in to make a seemingly impossible marriage system fairly workable. As the documents show, much of the testimony regarded not only actual witnessing of the contract but also "public voice and fame" about whether or not a marriage had taken place. The latter evidence was not in itself technically valid proof of a marriage, but both ecclesiastical officials and lay witnesses saw it as important corroboration of other testimony.

Some cohabiting couples never married, although this was frowned on both by the Church and by those who lived around them. Although it is unclear how many lived together without benefit of matrimony, we do know that neighbors disapproved and that local secular courts vigorously pressured some sexually active couples to marry. Extramarital sex was not socially acceptable, but it was also well known that intercourse was not in itself equivalent to marriage in canon law: only consent made a marriage. Thus, although the church court sometimes wanted to know whether a couple had had sexual intercourse, those being prosecuted knew that, without intention to marry, intercourse and consequent birth of children meant nothing legally (see case no. 3). As women bore the children from such unions, it was frequently they who attempted to pressure the men to marry them, and they were often supported in this by public opinion, both male and female. But if a man could resist such pressure, and it was not easy, he had no legal obligation to "make an honest woman" of his lover.

The ways in which testimony was manipulated also show awareness of church law and willingness to use the courts to individual advantage. Witnesses all too often perjured themselves, sometimes for payment, sometimes "out of love" for one of the litigants, sometimes, perhaps, because of pressure from an employer or other person in authority (see case nos. 13 and 14). Lawyers representing one of the parties in a suit were known to instruct deponents how to bear false witness. The common practice of paying witnesses' expenses raised the problem of where to draw the line between legitimate expenses and buying testimony.

The relationship between laypeople and the courts (both ecclesiastical or secular) reveals an interesting dialectic between competing interests attempting to use the apparatus available to obtain their goals. While the Church authorities who controlled the courts might appear to have the advantage, as they were, in a sense, makers as well as interpreters of the law, they did not have all the power, especially if witnesses were willing to disregard the fundamental rule that they tell the truth.

Courtship and Marriage Customs

Marriage in London had a special aspect: because so many young people came to London to work while they were in their teens, they often made their first marriages while living away from their parents and other family members. This perhaps allowed them more autonomy than their country cousins, but by no means were they left to make the momentous decision to marry or not to marry on their own. Those marrying for the second or even third time often made their choices more independently, although rarely without advice or help, especially in the case of women (see case no. 1). Historians have tended to focus on three categories of people having influence on a marriage: the principals themselves, the parents or guardians of the principals, and their manorial lords. By the fifteenth century, the influence of lords had all but disappeared, even on the manors, and they had never held sway in the towns. For many young people living in London, parents also were of little consideration, since they lived too far away to supervise or to advise. But the preliminaries to marriage in late medieval London show that, even if parents and lords were out of the picture or the parties were marrying for a second or third time, others would step in to make sure that this critical life decision was made sensibly. The people who lived around a couple, their relatives, friends, neighbors, and employers, assisted, prodded, and acted as intermediaries in order to make, or break, a proposed marriage.

Many people were involved in some way in the making of a marriage. The most important, of course, were the man and woman themselves. The depositions show that in fifteenth-century London, below the highest levels of the merchant elite (where the courtship of children, especially daughters, was very closely supervised), young people routinely chose prospective mates for themselves through the normal course of social interaction. Young men and women, often working as servants and apprentices, met one another in their everyday working world; as they went about their business, they often went in and out of other houses and shops, and along the way they came to know other young people. Deponents frequently mentioned taverns as places where people socialized with their friends and neighbors, courting and having celebratory drinks (see case no. 5). Feast-days, festivals, and market-days were also social events, for which people wore their best clothes and ate special meals. All these provided opportunities for people to find a mate.

The late age at which people first married in fifteenth-century England facilitated this relatively free marriage market. Most historians think that below elite social levels, late medieval English women and men married for the first time in their mid-twenties, that they usually chose spouses close in age to themselves, and that they established their own household, rather than moving in with the bride's or the groom's parents. This has been labelled a Northern European marriage pattern, in contrast to the pattern in Southern Europe, where men aged about thirty tended to marry women in their mid-to-late teens. As English men and women often moved away from home and started to work seriously when they were between twelve and fourteen, this left a long period of adolescence, when young people were neither children nor fully adults, which came with marriage.

Whether young men and women were normally sexually active during this long adolescence is not clear. In some cases in the church courts, witnesses deposed that a couple was known to sleep together, but in others it seems that consummation was assumed to come after, not before, a contract of marriage (see case no. 12). The risks of pregnancy in an age with no effective birth control may have inhibited many. Civic ordinances and anxiety about reputation indicate that sexual morals may have become stricter in the last half of the fifteenth century than they had been before, especially for women. Defamation suits show that reputation, a most precious possession in late medieval society, centered around chastity for women and honesty for men (see case nos. 19 and 22). Young men, less worried about their chastity, may have found an alternative to abstinence in commerce with prostitutes.

Economically, the period before marriage was also a time of transition. Both young men and young women spent this period trying to accumulate goods and skills for their marriage. Many young men were apprentices to a trade through their adolescence, living with a master and learning the secrets of the craft; by their early-to-mid twenties they were qualified and ready to head their own household. Young women only rarely entered apprenticeships by the end of the fifteenth century; most were live-in domestic servants from their mid-teens until their marriage. They, too, prepared for the time they would enter into their husband's household: a bride was often expected to provide a substantial dowry upon marriage, usually at least partly saved up from her wages while working as a servant, and the skills she had learned during her adolescence would help both to keep her household running and to supplement the household income through part-time work such as spinning and brewing ale.

P. J. P. Goldberg has recently hypothesized that the second half of the fifteenth century saw a significant downturn in economic opportunites for women and that this decline affected women's marriage choices. Earlier in the century, a buoyant urban economy had provided many opportunities for female employment; as a consequence, with many options open to them, women often chose to postpone marriage or not to marry at all. But with the contraction of the economy in the later fifteenth century, women were excluded from most types of employment. Their economic options upon reaching adulthood were, as a result, restricted to dependence within marriage or, with little other choice, poverty or prostitution. In the light of this theory, the women in the cases here had few alternatives but to marry. The importance women placed on the approval and advice of others (as we will see below) may reflect more caution and less independence than women had exercised seventy-five years before.

17

Introduction

In the second half of the fifteenth century courtship was not a private affair between two individuals only; it was a matter of much wider concern. It often involved many other parties, playing both informal and formal roles in bringing the courtship to fruition. Families, especially parents if they were still alive, were particularly important in dispensing advice and giving consent. But sons and daughters were not treated in the same way. While young men often acted independently in their marriage choices, young women were more reliant on and subject to parental consent in making this pivotal decision (see case nos. 1, 9, 10). This may be related to the fact that parents often provided some share of the woman's dowry, thus making daughters more dependent than sons on their parents' approval. Girls were also socialized to be less independent than boys, prefiguring the relative status of wives and husbands: wives were to obey and rely upon their husbands, who were to become heads of their households and the main decision-makers in the family. Parental influence over marriage was by no means absolute, but a child who married contrary to parents' wishes could expect repercussions ranging from displeasure to disinheritance and disownment.

Parental and familial involvement in the marriage decision was often not possible for young people in London. Mortality rates meant that many were orphaned by the time they were in their twenties, while others lived far away from their families (see case no. 12). But young people were not cast adrift to marry freely without advice or consultation: other networks tended to fill this need. Employers, especially, acted as substitute parents, and in some cases their approval of a marriage was considered to be as important as that of parents, even when parents were near at hand (see case no. 2). Employers also saw it as part of their moral duty to make sure that servants, especially female servants, did not partake in unsavory relationships.

Friends were also part of the network upon which a person considering marriage relied for advice and help. An individual's circle of friends could include both relations beyond the immediate family—cousins, uncles, aunts—and people unrelated by blood or marriage, simply those who had a close relationship with an individual or his or her family. A mutual friend usually handled the delicate matter of sending gifts to a potential lover and reported back to the giver how the gift had been received. Often even marriage proposals were conveyed through an intermediary rather than directly (see case no. 1). People also valued the advice of friends, stating that they wished to confer with them before making any firm decision regarding a marital contract.

But marriage was more than a personal, familial, or household matter in fifteenth-century England: as the foundation of the social system, it was considered to be of community concern as well. The wider community had both informal and formal means by which it encouraged or pressured men and women to conform to accepted norms and standards. If a couple was engaged in a sexual relationship without any moves towards marriage, those around them might bring informal pressure to bear. For instance, a deputation of the senior men of the neighborhood might question a man about the nature of his relationship with a certain woman. If such encounters were unsuccessful in persuading a man or a woman to do the right thing, then more formal means existed. The leaders of the neighborhood community might bring a case of fornication, adultery, or bigamy to the attention of the church courts. The local secular courts of the city (called ward moots) also called fornicators and adulterers before them and coerced them to marry or desist (see case nos. 21 and 23). Such moral issues were of common concern.

The community, in such cases, was governed by older men of respectable position, the patriarchs. Medieval patriarchy (literally "father-rule") was wider than a father's governance of his biological offspring. Fathers had special hegemony over their families, recognized in law and theory, but paternal power was echoed and buttressed by the paternalistic authority exercised generally by respectable older men, the fathers of the community. Senior men had the duty and the privilege to govern and to ensure the proper working of social relationships within their sphere of action. The maintenance of the community and the marital bond that, in many ways, was at its heart were their responsibility.

The most public and official aspects of the regulation of marriage and related issues—such as considering cases of fornicators before a local tribunal, or presiding over a domestic wedding as a master of ceremonies—were reserved for men. But women, too, played important roles in some cases, especially in informal ways, such as the conveying of gifts. Formal roles were less often their purview, although in the absence of men they could be called upon. When fathers were dead, mothers had a great deal of authority over children, especially daughters, and their consent was as eagerly sought as that of fathers (see case no. 10). Similarly, the mistresses of female servants were asked for their approval of a marriage choice. But women's influence was often more informal and secondary than men's: if there was a man in the picture, a father or male employer, his advice or consent was much more likely to be sought than a woman's.

Courtship and the negotiations leading up to marriage

consisted of a series of subtle and not-so-subtle signals sent back and forth between a marriageable man and a marriageable woman. The depositions often tell us about the climactic stages of this social dance. Gender norms dictated that men usually took the first and subsequent steps and that women reacted rather than acted; women could accept or refuse. This did not mean that everyone followed the rules, but those who broke them ran the risk of accusations of inappropriate behavior. Women who took direct action, for instance, were seen as, and often were, desperate. Most of the cases in the depositions of women directly taking the initiative in a proposal of marriage involved women who had borne several children by a man and who had been left with little choice but to attempt to persuade him to marry her (see case no. 3). This does not mean that women were unable to influence events or that they had no means to reach a desired end, but the most successful action for women was that which was cloaked in a passive guise. And in some ways the control that women could exercise in their reactive role, in being able to accept or reject, was in itself a considerable power.

The other point in a woman's life when she experienced power was in her widowhood, should she survive her husband. Widows were the only women who were not theoretically subject to a man, and while many suffered from poverty and all were still restricted from public life, some widows commanded substantial wealth and exercised considerable autonomy. This stage was often transitory, as wealthy widows in particular were likely to remarry and were required by law to hand over their wealth to their new husbands. In some cases, the power of widows was much greater than that of a young woman marrying for the first time: if she was wealthy, many might compete for her hand and she could play one off against another, as did Maude Knyff and Agnes Twytynge (case nos. 15 and 16). Widows were women of experience and maturity, and the depositions show that some of them were not shy about asserting their will.

Bound up in marriage, both in its legal and its social aspects, was a sense of tradition. People felt that there was a proper way to do things, the way it had been done before. Many marriages followed a certain pattern, and it seems clear that part of the negotiation process in the making of this intimate human tie was the unspoken motive behind and response to certain ritual actions, actions that were assigned meanings other than their explicit ones. But the meaning of social rituals was not always agreed upon by participants.

Gift-giving was particularly important in courtship ritual. The most common gifts were rings (still a potent marital symbol today), gloves, kerchiefs, and gold coins. Presents were exchanged by a courting couple, sometimes before a contract was made and frequently at the time of the actual contract. The gifts themselves were symbols of the contract, and they were invested with specific meaning by both the donor and the recipient. Sometimes disagreement arose about the meaning: a woman attempting to disavow that she had contracted with a man might deny that the kerchief he had given her was given to her "as from a husband to a wife." The gift was not in question in cases like this, but the spirit in which it was given and received was debated (see case no. 3).

In some cases, the parties indicated interest in a more direct way: one might ask another if he or she was interested in marriage. Men most often took the direct approach, as befitted their active role in the courtship. Many courtships were probably undertaken in this way, but the depositions indicate that another common pattern was to ask the crucial questions through intermediaries (see case no. 1). In one case, a London man named Robert asked his friend William to question Lucy whether she was committed to another man, and if she was not, if she was interested in Robert. William then relayed back to Robert her reply, that she was free of commitments and agreeable to speak and drink with him. The couple was then able to begin courting, knowing that each partner was, at least in theory, interested in the other.

The depositions indicate that a good deal of serious courting took place over food and drink, the customary center of social life in fifteenth-century England. Many testified that couples had conversations about marriage and other matters while sitting around a table, eating or drinking. Often this was in the woman's home or that of her employer, usually in the hall (where meals were taken), and sometimes in the local tavern. Other people were often present, and, as mentioned above, couples were often careful to have their conclusive conversations about making a marriage contract in the company of others, for greater openness and publicity.

The issue that has perhaps most interested historians in looking at medieval marriage has been the question of love. Some early work by historians of marriage and the family (Lawrence Stone has been most influential) propounded the theory that before the modern period people did not experience the emotion that we label romantic love, or at least that they did not experience it or expect it within marriage. These historians see medieval and early modern marriage choices as based solely on mercenary and political motives. Marriage choices were, in such a view, controlled mainly by parents, who saw their children's unions as means of increasing family income and stature. One married for money, power, and progeny, but not out of any personal affection.

Other historians have reacted against this theory. Scholars of medieval canon law have drawn attention to the importance that the medieval Church placed on the consent of the two individuals marrying. Parents could not marry off their children without any thought to their wishes, because the principals themselves had to give their free consent for any marriage to be valid. This idea of consent, they think, led to a marital system where choice of spouses was made freely. Alan Macfarlane, looking at marriage from the perspective of the birth of English individualism, similarly hypothesizes that the late Middle Ages saw the birth of a new style of marriage, which he calls love marriage, where individuals married without any concern for the thoughts or wishes of others.

These two branches of the debate on love and marriage in the pre-modern period have tended to see a rigid dichotomy between individual free choice in marriage (or marriage for love) and control of marriage choice by the family (marriage for political or financial reasons). Most medieval and early modern historians have rejected the views of Stone and others in his school: as the sources here show, "love" was certainly part of the vocabulary of marriage, and these and other sources show that it was of prime consideration in making a marriage choice. But this need not lead us to accept the direct opposite point of view, that marriages were made without any consideration of other factors beside love and without any participation by other parties beside the principals. The records clearly show the roles that family, employers, and friends played in all parts of the courtship. It can, indeed, be argued that late medieval Londoners perceived that a happy marriage was a suitable marriage; personal compatibility was part of the equation, but those considering marriage might also assess proper economic standing, family connections, and capability to have children.

Not only did the families of people wishing to marry think this but so also, evidently, did the principals themselves. Both men and women, young and old, internalized patriarchal norms, especially the idea that older people, particularly men, were wise about the ways of the world. To do the right thing, not to mention the wise thing, was to marry with the advice of parents, relatives, and friends. Margery Sheppard of London said in 1486 what many others, especially women, repeated during their courtships: "I will do as my father will have me; I will never have none against my father's will." Both men and women, and perhaps women to a greater extent, were conditioned to believe that happiness depended on choosing an appropriate spouse with the consent or advice of a parent or guardian. Sometimes free choice in marriage was to prefer to abide by the wishes of others.

Depositions and Late Medieval London

Depositions in fifteenth-century marriage cases can incidentally provide us with a great deal of information about other facets of late medieval London life. The formulaic biographical details recorded for each witness, for instance, reveal fundamental assumptions underlying late medieval social organization. Men were classified by their occupation, suggesting that this was a vital part of their identity. For women, on the other hand, their marital or family status was recorded. This encapsulates what many historians have noted about gender identities in the late Middle Ages—that men's was primarily occupation-associated while women's was related to their function within the family. Both reflect the work customarily performed by the two sexes: in the urban environment, for instance, households were organized around the trade or craft of the male head of the household. Men often associated socially and politically with others of their trade or craft, and their occupations sometimes determined even the location of their houses. Work of the women in the family, as well as other members of the household, both male and female servants, served to complement that of husband or father: women ran the household, cared for children, sometimes assisted in the trade or craft, and, if they had time, worked at a part-time job such as spinning or brewing. But even if a woman had an occupation, her primary identity was not her work status but her place in the family, whether unmarried woman, wife, or widow.

The ascription of literacy to a deponent also reveals important information about reading and writing in the dawn of the print era. Literacy is difficult to define even today, and we are not always sure what a designation of literacy meant in the Middle Ages. Many historians have hypothesized that literacy rates were rising steadily in the later Middle Ages, especially the fifteenth century, but others have challenged this view, contending that literacy was still relatively rare. The depositions here support the more pessimistic perspective. Men of higher-status trades and crafts or those styled "gentleman" were more likely to be able to read, but even they were not always literate. Perhaps even more revealing is that women were usually not even asked if they could read, and this detail was normally omitted from their biographical information altogether. It is possible that below elite social levels, where women as well as men were taught by private tutors, women were only rarely able to become literate. Reading ability was acquired in the Middle Ages primarily for economic reasons, and it was men's work—and then only higher-status men's work—that required it, and it was often taught in work training. Women had little reason and even less opportunity to learn to read, and it appears that the ecclesiastical courts simply assumed women were illiterate and saw no reason to record it. They could be wrong—in one case from the London Consistory Court in 1471 a sixty-year-old widow, Maude Radclyffe, spoke in her testimony about reading a document.

A last biographical detail—current and previous places and length of residence—is not always recorded, but the examples we have illustrate the remarkable mobility of the late medieval population. Both urban and rural people moved about a good deal in the course of their lives, most often within a twenty-five mile radius of their place of birth, but larger cities, such as London, drew their immigrant populations from a larger area. Servants, especially, who made up a significant proportion of urban populations, tended to be immigrants.

Court Procedure

Some technical information about the courts and the role of the depositions in marital litigation will be useful in understanding and interpreting the documents.

Various levels of church courts within each English diocese heard marriage cases. Depositions from the two books studied here relate mostly to marriage cases, although other records indicate that marital litigation made up only a relatively small part of all suits brought before church courts.

Introduction

In the course of the sixteenth century, documents similar to those found here recorded fewer marriage cases and many more concerning defamation.

The bishop's highest court was the Consistory Court, from which most of the depositions translated here come. Its judge was called the bishop's Official, who was a man university-trained in canon and civil law. A scribe or registrar recorded proceedings of the court. Litigants were assisted through the legal intricacies of the court by lawyers who were called advocates, usually university graduates in law, or proctors, often not formally trained.

The Commissary Court was a lower-level court, presided over by a commissary-general. Although the procedure in this court was probably somewhat less formal, the recording of the depositions there was done in much the same way as in the Consistory Court. While scribes recorded testimony from witnesses in both Consistory and Commissary Courts in deposition books, they used separate books to record appearances before the court and the sentences from the cases. Unfortunately, both sorts of books survive only in limited number, and they do not match up: sentences do not survive for the cases for which we have depositions, and vice versa. Other church courts, such as archdeaconry courts and the Court of Arches, an archdiocesan appellate court, also heard marriage cases in London, but very little documentation survives from them.

This pamphlet provides translations of what are perhaps the most interesting records from fifteenth-century church courts, the testimony recorded in the deposition books. The presiding judge usually examined the witnesses (appearing for either the plaintiff or the defendant) individually, in a private house (the house of the scribe was frequently used), or in a room in St. Paul's Cathedral or elsewhere. In each case he questioned the witnesses according to a series of articles, questions, and charges that was set out by the lawyers of the parties involved in the suit to the court. A principal in a case could also appear to answer the allegations of his or her opponent. At the actual hearing, the scribe probably took notes that he later wrote in a more formal style into the books we now have. He did not record the actual article or question to which the witness responded in the deposition; presumably, anyone wishing to refer to the deposition was assumed to have a copy of those documents as well. The clerk translated the depositions, which the witnesses gave in English, into Latin. In the course of the fifteenth century, ecclesiastical court clerks began more frequently to insert English words, especially in quotations, reflecting the legal importance of knowing the exact words spoken in marriage contracts and defamations.

The initial parts of a deponent's testimony established the witness's identity and his or her credibility in the case. The scribe identified the witnesses by name, occupation (usually only in the case of men), marital status (in the case of women), and place of residence. He also recorded literacy, in the case of men. A person's legal condition, free or unfree, verified eligibility to testify, since, theoretically, an unfree person (a serf) could not testify before a court. By the second half of the fifteenth century, though, few English people were still of servile status, and so this question was mostly a formality. The clerk also noted the age of the deponent, as only adults (apparently defined as sixteen and older) could testify. Finally, the witnesses stated how long they had known the parties in the case. This last piece of information presumably showed that the deponent was in a position to know intimate details about the litigants' lives.

The questions witnesses were asked in marriage cases centered around points essential to the case and the canon law of marriage, but the court gave witnesses some freedom to tell fairly lengthy stories. In most marriage cases, the most important issue for the court was usually whether or not the principals had properly exchanged consent. Sometimes priority was the matter at hand: which exchange of consent came first? At other times, the exact words spoken and whether they constituted free and unconditional consent were in question. The court was also interested, however, in the events that surrounded the actual exchange of words, since other factors could influence whether or not both parties participated of their own free will. Suits in which consent was not the question—for instance, divorce *a mensa et thoro* on the basis of cruelty—obviously elicited other sorts of questioning and testimony.

The depositions in marriage cases elucidate much about love and marriage in the everyday lives of ordinary Londoners. The testimony reveals that the marital system was complex, but we can learn a great deal about how spouses were chosen, how couples courted, and how they married one another. Perhaps the most striking element to a modern observer is the importance of parish, neighborhood, and community in fifteenth-century London, especially as regards marriage. This basic social tie was more than a personal affair.

Introduction

Note on Translations:

The depositions come from two manuscripts: London, Greater London Record Office [abbreviated as GLRO], MS DL/C/205, Consistory Court of London Deposition Book, 1467–76; and London, Guildhall Library [abbreviated as GL], MS 9065, Commissary Court of London Deposition Book, 1489–97. The records are translated from Latin. When the scribes used English in the original deposition (indicated by italics in the text) I have retained the medieval spelling. The scribes employed two Middle English letters we have since lost: þ (which we write as 'th') and ȝ (now usually 'y' or 'gh'). Scribes originally recorded names in the depositions with the first name translated into Latin (so that John is Johannes) and the surname in English. Here I have translated the first name into a modern English equivalent and the last name I have kept as spelled in the original.

The year in medieval England began on March 25 (the feast of the Annunciation of the Blessed Virgin), but the dates here have been adjusted so that the year begins on January 1.

Suggestions for Further Reading

The following is a selection of recent scholarship on medieval and early modern marriage, oriented especially to England.

For general bibliography, see *Domestic Society in Medieval Europe: A Select Bibliography*, ed. Michael M. Sheehan and Jacqueline Murray (Toronto: Pontifical Institute of Mediaeval Studies Press, 1990), part of a larger and more comprehensive bibliography that is forthcoming. Good introductions to marriage in the Middle Ages are Christopher Nugent Lawrence Brooke, *The Medieval Idea of Marriage* (Oxford: Oxford University Press, 1989), and Frances and Joseph Gies, *Marriage and the Family in the Middle Ages* (New York: Harper & Row, 1987). For families, see David Herlihy, *Medieval Households* (Cambridge, Mass.: Harvard University Press, 1985). Beatrice Gottlieb, *The Family in the Western World from the Black Death to the Industrial Age* (New York: Oxford University Press, 1993), covers the early modern period. Gene Brucker, *Giovanni and Lusanna: Love and Marriage in Renaissance Florence* (Berkeley: University of California Press, 1986), is an interesting study of a marriage case in the very different society of fifteenth-century Italy. Barbara A. Hanawalt's *Growing Up in Medieval London: The Experience of Childhood in History* (New York: Oxford University Press, 1993) is a vivid account of Londoners' lives from birth to first marriage in the fourteenth and fifteenth centuries.

No recent general book-length treatments of marriage in

medieval England have yet appeared. Barbara A. Hanawalt's *The Ties that Bound: Peasant Families in Medieval England* (New York: Oxford University Press, 1986) and Judith M. Bennett's *Women in the Medieval English Countryside: Gender and Household in Brigstock Before the Plague* (New York: Oxford University Press, 1987) both have chapters on marriage and the peasantry. Joel Thomas Rosenthal's *Patriarchy and Families of Privilege in Fifteenth-Century England* (Philadelphia: University of Pennsylvania Press, 1991) discusses marriage among the gentry and nobility.

Much work on medieval marriage has concentrated on the legal aspect. For a guide to the canon law of marriage and sexuality, see James A. Brundage, *Law, Sex, and Christian Society in Medieval Europe* (Chicago: University of Chicago Press, 1987). On English church courts, see especially Richard Helmholz, *Marriage Litigation in Medieval England* (London and New York: Cambridge University Press, 1974); other important works include Michael M. Sheehan, "Formation and Stability of Marriage in Fourteenth-Century England: Evidence of an Ely Register," *Mediaeval Studies* 33 (1971): 228–63, and Richard M. Wunderli, *London Church Courts and Society on the Eve of the Reformation* (Cambridge, Mass.: Medieval Academy of America, 1981).

The role of marriage in the economic lives of medieval people has also been explored. See the work of Bennett and Hanawalt, above. The recent publications of P. J. P. Goldberg, especially *Women, Work, and Life Cycle in a Medieval Economy: Women in York and Yorkshire, c. 1300–1520* (Oxford: Clarendon Press; New York: Oxford University Press, 1992), are important contributions that use material similar to that translated here. See also the essays by Goldberg,

Suggestions for Further Reading

Richard M. Smith, and P. P. A. Biller in *Woman is a Worthy Wight: Women in English Society, c. 1200–1500*, ed. P. J. P. Goldberg (Gloucester and Wolfeboro, N.H.: Alan Sutton, 1992). L. R. Poos, *A Rural Society After the Black Death: Essex, 1350–1525* (Cambridge and New York: Cambridge University Press, 1991), explores the economic lives of people living just north of London and uses the Deposition Books translated here as sources.

The field of marriage in early modern England is an active one. Two historians, Lawrence Stone (see especially *The Family, Sex, and Marriage in England, 1500–1800* [New York: Harper Torchbooks, 1979]) and Alan Macfarlane (*Marriage and Love in England: Modes of Reproduction, 1300–1840* [Oxford and New York: Blackwell, 1986]) have written wide-ranging and influential histories of marriage and the family, although their interpretations of medieval marriage have not generally been accepted by specialists. Other useful surveys include Ralph A. Houlbrooke, *The English Family, 1450–1700* (London and New York: Longman, 1984); Martin Ingram *Church Courts, Sex, and Marriage in England, 1570–1640* (Cambridge and New York: Cambridge University Press, 1987); and Eric Josef Carlson, *Marriage and the English Reformation* (Oxford and Cambridge, Mass.: Blackwell, 1994). Recent and important journal publications include Diana O'Hara, "'Ruled by My Friends': Aspects of Marriage in the Diocese of Canterbury, c. 1540–1570," *Continuity and Change* 6 (1991): 9–41; Diana O'Hara, "The Language of Tokens and the Making of Marriage," *Rural History* 3, no. 1 (1992): 1–40; Peter Rushton, "Property, Power and Family Networks: The Problem of Disputed Marriage in Early Modern England," *Journal of Family History* 11 (1986): 205–19; Ralph Houlbrooke, "The

Making of Marriage in Mid-Tudor England: Evidence from the Records of Matrimonial Contract Litigation," *Journal of Family History* 10 (1985): 339–52; and Miranda Chaytor, "Household and Kinship: Ryton in the Late Sixteenth and Early Seventeenth Centuries," *History Workshop Journal* 10 (1980): 25–60.

Depositions from Marital Litigation

Courtship and the Making of a Marriage Contract

1. John Brocher v. Joan Cardif alias Peryn (GL, MS 9065, fols. 22r–24r)

> *In this case, John Brocher sues Joan Cardif because she has not fulfilled the contract of marriage he claims she made. (In all the cases, the first-named party in the heading is suing and the other is being sued.) The depositions attesting to the contract show mediators playing a prominent role, both in the negotiations before marriage and in the making of the contract itself. Note also the importance Joan Cardif places on her mother's consent, although Joan is a widow and, thus, theoretically independent.*

4 July [149?]

John Miller of Enfield [Essex], where he has lived for fifty years, weaver, illiterate, of free condition, seventy years old. He has known John Brocher for twenty years and Joan Cardif for four years. To the first and second articles, he says that on the Tuesday before last Easter, this deponent, at John Brocher's desire and request, went to Joan's house at Walthamstow [Essex]. On John's behalf, this deponent gave Joan some fish and told her that John was coming right away with certain other people and that she should prepare the fish for their dinner. Joan received the fish happily. Afterwards, she came up to this deponent, who was then in the stable,

37

and consulted him about whether John would be a husband for her. He answered her that if she could find it in her heart to love him as her husband, John would be hers forever. They discussed the substance of John's goods and debts, and this deponent told her that John's debts did not exceed 40s. Joan asked him then to pay 40s. out of her money (which at that time was in this deponent's hands) into the hands of John's creditors, so that John Brocher would not have to sell his goods. Then John Brocher, Thomas Lee, and John Monk came to the house. After they had dined in the hall of the house, John Monk asked Joan whether she was free from all contracts of marriage and whether she could find it in her heart to love John as her husband. She answered yes, by her faith. John Monk said further in English, *"Johan, how sest thou, wilt thou have this man,"* gesturing toward John, *"to thi husband?"* Joan responded, *"Ye, by my feith."* Then John, at the instruction of John Monk, said to Joan, taking her by his right hand, *"I, John, take the, Johan, for my weddid wif, by my feith and trouth."* Joan responded, *"I wil have you to my weddid husbond by my feith, but I will not pliʒt you feith and trouth till after Ester, that I cover [it] before my moder."* Afterward John, on that same day, gave to Joan a belt decorated with silver. Moreover John told this deponent that he and Joan would come to an agreement the Wednesday of Easter week, when they would meet in this deponent's house in Enfield. On that Wednesday, John and Joan appeared in his house before this deponent and his wife. John asked Joan whether she wished to make permanent the words she had spoken at her own house in Walthamstow; she responded yes, by her faith, and that she wished to have him as her husband. Then John gave to Joan a certain kerchief which she gratefully accepted from him, kissing him and tying the kerchief around her neck. This deponent's wife, Joan's mother, said to Joan, *"On that condicion I geve you goddis blessing and myne to gedir,"* which this deponent saw and heard himself. To the third article, he says that at the time of this contract, John sent to Joan eight parcels of his chattels, which she possesses presently, as he believes. . . . To the fourth article, he says that there was public voice and fame about the contract of marriage in Enfield and Walthamstow. To the first question, . . . he says that John asked this deponent to be his friend and to offer his blessing for taking Joan as his wife, and this deponent conceded to him that he wished him well in this matter, but that he would not make other solications towards Joan. . . . To the fourth question, he says that he does not love one party more than the other and he wishes that Joan would have John as her husband because she gave her faith in this matter, as he says.

Katherine Miller, wife of John Miller, of the parish of Enfield, where she has lived for four years, of free condition, fifty-three years old, sworn etc. She has known John Brocher for four years, and Joan Peryn, her natural daughter, from the time of her birth. To the first and second articles, she says that she heard from her husband and from others that John and Joan had contracted marriage between them in Joan's house during Lent. She says that on the Wednesday in the last Easter Week John and Joan were present in the home of her husband at Enfield when John Brocher, in the presence of this deponent and her husband, asked Joan whether she wished to make permanent by matrimonial words what she had previously promised before John Miller and others at Walthamstow. She responded thus, *"Ye, by my feith and my trouth,"* and then John gave her a certain kerchief which she took and put around her neck. This deponent, joyful about this matter, gave Joan her blessing. . . . To the second and third questions, . . . she says that when Joan praised John and consulted the deponent whether she should have him as her husband, this deponent said that John was an honest man and suitable for her, but she did not make any other solicitations or efforts, as she says. To the fourth question, she says that . . . she would prefer that Joan accept John as her husband. She does not want Joan to have victory in this case because she believes in her conscience that then she would betray her oath.

2. **John Bedeman v. Agnes Nicholas** (GLRO, MS DL/C/205, fols. 56v–57v)

The contract in this case is being contested by Agnes Nicholas, although her father testifies in John Bedeman's favor. Again the contract was made with the help of a mediator—a man unrelated to either party, presumably a friend of the family, who instructs the parties how to say their vows. The second deposition, from the woman's father, tells us about an earlier stage in the courtship. Note the important role played by John Capron, Agnes Nicholas's master, even though her father was present.

23 March 1470

William Prudmay, living in the household of the Duchess of York, literate, of free condition, fifty-six years old. He says that he has known John Bedeman for a year and Agnes Nicholas for twelve years. To the first and second articles of the statement, he says that on a certain feast day around the last feast of St. Michael [29 Sept.], whether before or after he does not know, he was present in the home of Thomas Nicholas, in the parish of St. Botulph without Aldersgate, London, after noon on that day. This deponent, Thomas Nicholas, and Joan his wife sat together in the hall, talking together about contracting marriage between John Bedeman and Agnes Nicholas, who were also there present. At length this deponent, among other things that were discussed between them, asked John Bedeman whether he could find in his heart to have Agnes, there present, as his wife. John responded yes, by his faith. In a similar manner he asked Agnes whether she could find it in her heart to have John as her husband, and she responded yes, by her faith. They all got up and went out into the garden, and there in the garden, beneath a vine, this deponent asked Agnes whether she could find in her heart to have John Bedeman, there present, as her husband, and she answered yes, by her faith. Then this deponent had her take John by the hand, and he asked John whether he could find it in his heart to have Agnes as his wife, and he said yes, by his faith. They unclasped their hands and kissed one another, and they drank good beer.

Thomas Nycholas of the parish of St. Botulph without Aldersgate, London, illiterate, of free condition, sixty-five years old and more. He says that he has known John Bedeman for a year and Agnes Nicholas since her birth, as Agnes is his daughter. To the first and second articles, he says that as far as the spirit and the deeds, he agrees with the testimony of William Prudmay, examined above. He adds this, that on the last feast of the Apostles Peter and Paul [29 June], this deponent, his wife, and John Bedeman were dining together with John Capron, goldsmith, who lives in Cheap. After dinner, John Capron said to John Bedeman, "You are trying to marry one of my girls," and John Bedeman answered yes. John Capron called Agnes, saying to her, "Take a penny from John Bedeman here present, and put the penny on the table," and she did it. Then he asked John Bedeman whether he could find it in his heart to have Agnes, there present, as his wife, and he answered yes, by his faith, in English, *"Yes, for sothe."* Next he asked Agnes if she could find it in her heart to have John Bedeman as her husband, and she answered, *"Yes, for sothe."* Asked who was there present and listening to these things, he said that John Capron, this deponent, his wife, John Bedeman, Agnes Nicholas, and another man whose name he does not know.

Exchange of Gifts

3. **Katherine Aber v. Robert Allerton** (GLRO, MS DL/C/205, fols. 150r–150v)

> *Gifts were frequently given and received in courtship and upon a contract of marriage. As such, they constituted evidence that a contract had been made. But it was the intention of the donor and of the recipient that was important and that ascribed meaning to the act and to the gift itself. Some deponents, however, attempted to persuade the court that the gifts they gave or received were not in the name of marriage.*

Depositions

Responses personally made by Robert Allerton, 2 May 1472

To the first charge, he says that Katherine Aber spoke to him many times about contracting marriage with her; when she spoke with him about it, he always denied that he wished to do this. Otherwise he and Katherine never discussed matters or spoke together, as he says. To the second charge, he denies all the contents in it. But he says that he often knew Katherine carnally and by her conceived a daughter, who is still alive. To the third charge, he says that on a certain day, which he does not now recall, this deponent deposited certain gold rings with Katherine. He asked for them back from Katherine, but she kept one of them and says that she doesn't want to return it but wants to keep it as a sign of his love, to claim this deponent as her husband. He says, however, that he gave it to her for fifteen shillings and a black gown and other things which he cannot now recall, and thus did not give it to her on the occasion of any marriage, as he says. To the fourth charge, he denies all the contents in it. But he says that Katherine at various times gave him two gold rings and another gilded with gold, and many pieces of *Rebeyn*, and forty-two shillings and six pence. He admits that he received similar things sent by her (recorded on a document given to the court by Katherine and read out loud at the time of this deponent's examination); he never received them from her, however, as from his wife or gave other things to her as to his wife, but only because of desire of his body and satisfying his lust.

Depositions

Rituals at Marriage

4. **Edmund Breme v. Petronilla Kember** (GLRO, MS DL/C/205, fols. 198v–199r)

The depositions usually give little indication about the wedding night, but this case reveals an almost ritualistic witnessing of the married couple in bed.

23 October 1473

Nicholas Maryot of the parish of St. Gregory, London, cook, illiterate, of free condition, forty years of age. He says that he has known Edmund Breme for a year and Petronilla Kember for twelve years. To the first and second articles, he says that on the third Sunday of Lent last past [21 March], it happened that this deponent was present at Petronilla Kember's house in Kensington, together with Margaret Maryot his wife. Around five o'clock in the afternoon, Edmund Breme and Petronilla Kember, sitting at the table in the parlor, discussed contracting marriage between them. At length Edmund called this deponent and Margaret his wife, who were at that time in the hall of the house, and asked them to bear witness about what would be said and done between him and Petronilla. At his request, this deponent, with his wife, entered into the parlor. After they had entered and talked about the idea of contracting marriage between them, Edmund took Petronilla by her right hand and said to her, "I take you, Petronilla, as my wife, and thereto I give you my faith." Immediately Petronilla said to him, "And I take you, Edmund, as my husband, and thereto I give you my faith," and they kissed one another. After these words had been spoken, on the same day between seven and eight o'clock, this deponent saw Edmund Breme and Petronilla

44

lying in a bed in a certain upper chamber of this house, both of them nude. This deponent happened to see this because his wife made certain preparations in the said chamber before they went to bed, and this deponent's wife was present at the time that they went to bed and called this deponent to the chamber, where he saw Edmund and Petronilla lying thus in the bed. They said to him, "Good night to you," and then this deponent left the room with his wife.

Location of the Exchange of Consent

5. **William Forster v. Ellen Grey** (GLRO, MS DL/C/205, fol. 165r)

> *Contracts occurred in many places, but most commonly in places of recreation: in the hall of the house, sitting by the fire, eating a meal, or, as this case shows, in a tavern.*

23 September 1472

Robert Jonson of the parish of St. Mary Aldermary, London, brother of Ellen Grey, illiterate, of free condition, twenty-four years old. He says that he has known William Forster for seven years and Ellen Grey from the time of her birth. To the first and second articles of the statement, he says that on Monday after the feast of the Epiphany [6 Jan.] two years ago, between the hours of eight and eleven in the morning, he was present in the tavern at the sign of the Greyhound in East Cheap, on a certain bench across from the door to the tavern. William Forster and Ellen Grey were sitting on the bench discussing contracting marriage between them, in the presence of this deponent, William Glenton now dead, Richard Barbour, a man named Abbot, and a man named Baron. During this conversation, this deponent said the following words to William Forster: "A little while ago I heard that you contracted marriage with Ellen Grey, my sister; tell me if this is true." William Forster affirmed that this was so. This deponent then said to William Forster, "So that this matter of which we speak be made more sure, say your vows again in my presence and in the presence of the others here, so that I and the other men here present can testify to the completeness of the marriage between you." After these words, William Forster took Ellen by her right hand and said to her, "I, William, take you, Ellen, as my wife, and thereto I give you my faith," and they unclasped their hands. Immediately Ellen took William by the hand and said to him, "And I, Ellen, take you, William, as my husband, and thereto I give you my faith." Then both the contracting parties and the other men named drank red and white wine.

6. **Alice Couper v. Henry Stowe** (GLRO, MS DL/C/205, fol. 105r)

> *In the Church's view, a marriage should be properly solemnized in a church. Traditionally, a contract of marriage was exchanged at the church door, perhaps to symbolize the Church's ambivalent attitude towards marriage or the liminal status of marriage as both a religious and a social bond. Afterwards, a nuptial mass was celebrated inside the church.*

8 April 1471

Alice Bonour, wife of Master John Bonour of the parish of St. Faith the Virgin, London, of free condition, fifty-four years of age. She says that she has known Alice Couper for twenty years and more and Henry Stowe for twelve years and more. . . . Questioned further, she says that she knows only that on a certain Sunday between the feast of All Saints [1 Nov.] and the first Sunday of Advent eleven years ago [30 Nov. 1460], exactly what day she cannot specify, she was present in the church of St. Clement situated in the city of Cambridge, where and when the curate of the church, whose name was said to be Damblet, recited certain matrimonial words in the solemnization of marriage there in the door of the said church, celebrated between Henry Stowe and Alice Couper. . . . After the solemnization, the priest entered into the church with Henry and Alice and celebrated a nuptial mass for them. This deponent also participated in the nuptial mass with Henry and Alice.

7. **Thomas Conyngham v. Joan Fordell** (GLRO, MS DL/C/205, fol. 140v)

The depositions show that sometimes contracts of marriage were exchanged inside the church, in the nave (where the congregation stood at mass) rather than at the door.

28 February 1472

Thomas Piers of the parish of St. Olave Old Jewry, London, tallow-chandler, literate, of free condition, twenty-nine years old and more. He has known Thomas Conyngham for two years and Joan Fordell for twenty years and Thomas Fordell for twenty-six years. Questioned further about the contents of the statement, he says that on a certain Sunday between the feasts of Easter [late March to late April] and St. John the Baptist [24 June], nineteen years ago and more as he believes, which day or which year he cannot otherwise specify, this deponent was present in the church of St. Stephen Walbrook, London, before noon of that day, between matins and high mass, when he saw and heard a priest . . . solemnizing marriage in the nave of the church between Thomas Fordell and Joan Fordell. . . . When the solemnization was completed and finished in the nave of the church according to the custom of the English Church, the couple followed the priest up the steps to the high altar, and there and then the priest celebrated the nuptial mass and did all the other things which are to be performed by the priest in that rite. This deponent offered in the nuptial mass with the couple.

The Domestic Contract followed by Banns

8. **James Whytyndon v. Agnes Rogers** (GLRO, MS DL/C/205, fols. 221r–223r)

This case shows the importance of banns, announcements of impending marriage between two individuals made from the pulpit of their parish church(es) three times before the solemnization. As the two depositions here show, the couple first contracted marriage by present consent in a domestic ceremony, and then asked the priest to issue banns.

Depositions

24 May 1474

Sir[2] Robert White, rector of the parish church of St. Ethelburga, city of London, where he has been rector for twenty-two years, of free condition, eighty years old. He says that he has known James Whytyngdon for ten years and Agnes Rogers from the feast of last Easter, as he says. To the first, second, third, fourth, and fifth articles of the statement, he says that he knows only that James Whytyngdon, on the day of Easter last past [April 10], came to him and asked him to proclaim banns of marriage between him and Agnes Rogers on the following Monday in this deponent's church. This deponent did as he was asked on the Monday, and immediately on that Monday after Vespers he came to Agnes Rogers' house and told her that he had on that day issued banns between her and James in the parish church, and she thanked him and was well contented with it. She then asked this deponent to issue the banns again on the following Sunday, which he did. . . . She asked him to issue them a third time the subsequent Sunday. He again did as he was asked, and when he told her that the banns had been proclaimed a third time, she thanked him profusely and showed him a happy face and drank to it. . . . To the sixth article, he says that . . . James and Agnes contracted marriage together and that marriage banns were issued between them three times in the parish of St. Ethelburga and in the parish of St. Mary at Axe, and that there was public voice and fame concerning it, as he says. To the fifth question, he says . . . that the said fame took its origin from the proclamations of banns, and the fame spread to almost all the people of those parishes because the banns were publicly issued between them in the aforesaid parishes.

Depositions

William Oldale of the parish of St. Christopher, city of London, where he has lived since last Easter. Before then, from the time of his birth, he lived at Coggeshall [Essex] with his father, except for two years, when he lived with a merchant named John Malter, girdler. Literate, of free condition, twenty-three years old, as he says, sworn as a witness, etc. He says that he has known James Whytyngdon for eighteen years and Agnes for a year and more, as he says. To the first and second articles of the statement, he says that on the feastday of St. Blaise [3 Feb.] last past, around two o'clock in the afternoon, this deponent was in the hall of Agnes's house, together with John Fuller, James, Agnes, and a girl of about fourteen. James and Agnes talked together about contracting marriage between them. At length Agnes, standing, first took James by his right hand and said to him, "I take you as my husband, and thereto I give you my faith." Then James, also standing, holding his hand in hers, said to her, "And I take you as my wife, and thereto I give you my faith." They then kissed one another, which this deponent testifies from his own sight and hearing.

Contracts Conditional on the Consent of Family Members

9. **Examination of Hugh Ford, Alice Ford, Richard Cordell, and Margery Ford** (GLRO, MS DL/C/205, fols. 136v–137v, 138v–139v)

Banns offered people in the congregation an opportunity to object to the marriage: not on any grounds, but on grounds of an impediment such as a previous marriage. When such an objection was made, the marriage was to be suspended and the case heard before a court. In this case, Margery Ford's parents objected to the banns ostensibly because Margery had not agreed to marry Richard Cordell (although it also appears as if they did not approve of the marriage).

Responses personally made by Hugh Ford, 6 February 1472

To the first, second, and third questions, he denies all contents. To the fourth question, he says that about two weeks ago he heard William Cordell and his wife Denise saying, in the presence of this deponent, that Margery Ford, this deponent's daughter, had received a gold ring and a pair of gloves from Denise's hands [on Richard's behalf]. He denies the other contents. . . . To the seventh question, he says that around the feast of St. Andrew [30 Nov.] last, and he cannot be more specific, this deponent came to the vicar of Enfield, who was in his church on a Sunday at the time of high mass, and said to him that in no way should he proclaim banns between Richard Cordell and Margery his daughter, until such a time as Richard and Margery are better agreed. Otherwise he did not object, as he says. He says in addition that he said these things on his own authority and not by anyone else's authority or command. Otherwise he did not molest Richard Cordell or bother him or have anyone else bother him, as he says. . . .

Responses personally made by Alice Ford

To the seventh question, she says that on a certain Saturday around the feast of St. Andrew last, which day exactly she cannot say, this deponent went to the vicar of Enfield, who was in his church, and spoke to him immediately after vespers, and asked him not to proclaim the banns of marriage between Richard Cordell and Margery, this deponent's daughter, until such a time as Richard and Margery are better agreed. Otherwise she did not object, as she says. She says moreover that she made this objection on Margery's authority and command, and not by anyone else's authority.

Responses personally made by Richard Cordell and Margery Ford, 8 February 1472

To the seventh charge, Richard says that Margery impeded and had her mother impede the public solemnization of their marriage before the church, and he says that he knows this because Margery's mother came to the vicar of Enfield with the intention of impeding the solemnization of marriage between them, and he saw this with his own eyes. Margery admits this. . . . To the ninth charge, Richard says that he procured the proclamation of marriage banns in Enfield. Margery says that she never procured them. . . . To the eleventh charge, . . . Margery, in response to a question, says that even if her parents gave their consent for her to marry Richard, she still would not give her consent, as she says.

10. **Elizabeth Isaak v. John Bolde** (GLRO, MS DL/C/205, fols. 131v–132v)

Some women made marriage contracts conditional on the consent of a family member (this was rarely the case with men). This case shows both a brother (only twenty) offering consent and a mother's blessing being sought.

Depositions

15 January 1472

Walter Isaak of the parish of St. Mary Bothaw, patten-maker, illiterate, of free condition, twenty years old and more. He says that he has known Elizabeth Isaak from the time of his ability to distinguish people and John Bolde for the last two years and a third. To the first and second articles, he says that on a certain Sunday three weeks after the feast of Pentecost a year ago [i.e., 1 July 1470], in the afternoon, this deponent was present in the house of William Case, situated in the parish of All Saints on the Wall, London, together with Elizabeth Isaak, John Bolde, and the wife of William Case and none others. John Bolde and Elizabeth talked about contracting marriage between them. At length John Bolde asked Elizabeth whether she could find it in her heart to have John as her husband, and she answered that she wished freely to have him as her husband if this deponent, her brother, would consent to it, and then this deponent gave them his consent. Then Elizabeth said to John, "I will have you as my husband, and forsake all other men for you, by my faith." John answered her, "And I will have you as my wife, and forsake all other women for you, by my faith." Afterward on a certain feast day within the week after the Sunday, this deponent was present in the house of William Case together with John Bolde and Elizabeth, where and when John Bolde, among other things communicated between them, said to Elizabeth, "Elizabeth, I will have you as my wife, and I will take you as my wife before the next feast of Pentecost." Elizabeth said to him, "I will have you as my husband, and will be governed by you." To the third article, he says that on Monday in Pentecost week a year ago [11 June 1470], this deponent and John Bolde were together in the parish of Weldham [unknown][3] in the house of

Humfrey Starkey, after noon, where and when in the presence of this deponent and Beatrice Isaak (Elizabeth's mother), John Bolde asked Beatrice's consent and good will, so that Beatrice would like John better, because he had taken Elizabeth as his wife, and Beatrice immediately gave him her good will. .... He says that after these words were spoken between them, John and Elizabeth ate, drank, and spoke together as man and wife, as this deponent saw many times.

Common Knowledge and Concern about Marriage

11. **John Holder v. Agnes Chambyrleyn** (GLRO, MS DL/C/205, fols. 114r, 125r)

Marriage was a subject of general concern and conversation among people living in medieval London. This case shows the common currency of rumors about marriage on the street. In the second deposition, reference is made to earlier depositions by William and Marion Phyppis. They had testified that they had witnessed a contract of marriage between John Holder and Agnes Chambyrleyn, even though according to Thomas Hert they had denied it only a few days before their depositions.

14 July 1471

Thomas Smyth, pewterer, of the parish of St. Alphage near Cripplegate, London, literate, of free condition, thirty-five years old. He says that he has known John Holder for four years and Agnes Chambyrleyn for twelve years. Questioned further concerning the contents in this statement, he says that he knows only that on a certain day around the beginning of Lent last past, which day he cannot say more certainly, this deponent met Agnes, who was then in the alley called Botulph Lane, next to Billingsgate. This deponent said to her, "Agnes, they tell me that you are the wife of John Holder and promised to him." She responded, "I am amazed that you know about this matter between him and me. I beg you not to tell my parents, because if you do, they will be angry with me; but I tell you plainly that he is my husband and I am promised to him." This deponent testifies about this from his own sight and hearing. He says moreover that within the last month, this deponent conveyed a gold angelet[4] to Agnes on behalf of John Holder, and Agnes received it happily, with a pleased look on her face, as it appeared to this deponent.

10 January 1472

Thomas Hert of the parish of St. Mary Colechurch, London, grocer, where he has lived for two years and more, before that time he lived in various places in the city of London for twelve years and more, literate, of free condition, about twenty-six years old. . . . He says that he has known Agnes Chambyrleyn for six years and John Holder for about five years. . . . To the second article, he says that on a certain Saturday in the month before the examination of William Phyppis and his wife Marion, as he believes, after noon on that day around three or four o'clock, he was present in his shop, situated in his house in the parish of St. Mary Colechurch. There and then he saw William Phyppis standing inside the shop and he said to him, "William, do you know of any marriage between John Holder and Agnes Chambyrleyn?" William responded, *"So helpe me good atte holy dome, I knowe non be twyxe hem, save only as Y here my wyf sey."* He says that there were present in that shop at the time these words were spoken, John Myddylton, who heard these words, and many others, whose names he cannot recite at present. He says moreover that about eight or nine days after this conversation with William Phippis, Marion Phyppis, his wife, on a certain day which he cannot specify, entered into the shop of this deponent to buy groceries from him. William Hert, this deponent's brother, said to Marion in this deponent's presence, "Marion, do you know about any marriage between John Holder and Agnes Chambyrleyn?" Marion immediately responded, *"So helpe me God atte holy dome, and by our lady, I knowe none."* Then William Hert asked Marion whether she would swear to this on a book, and Marion replied that she would swear to it on all the mass books of the world. There were present at this time and listening to this conversation this deponent, William Hert, John Rampsey, and no others.

Disputed Contracts: Attempting to Escape

12. **Agnes Whitingdon v. John Ely** (GL, MS 9065, fols. 10r–12r)

> *Many cases involved attempts to deny that a contract had been made. In this case, influential friends rallied around a young woman, without parents in the city to protect her interests, when a man attempted to disavow a contract he had made with her.*

John Ely's responses, 29 January 1487

   . . . He denies the second article of the statement, saying

that around the feast of St. Michael the Archangel [29 Sept.] last, a certain Hawkyn, Agnes's master, asked him if he wanted to have Agnes in marriage. This deponent said that he did not want to contract with Agnes without first knowing how much her friends were willing to give as her dowry. Then he proposed that a certain man named Robert ride to Agnes's parents to find out how much they would give as her dowry, but Agnes said that her father would be coming to London around the next feast of All Saints [1 Nov.]. So this deponent conceded that he would wait until that feast and give Agnes an answer then, and until that time he would not speak to her about such matters. He said moreover that he would like to have her as his wife if he could have with her five marks[5] by the feast of All Saints. To the third article, he says that after this conversation he lent to Agnes a pair of coral beads. . . . To the fifth charge, he denies any rumors [about their marriage].

29 January

John Roberd of the parish of St. Margaret Moses in Friday Street, London, where he has lived for four years, literate, of free condition, a cheesemonger, forty years old. He has known Agnes Whitingdon for two years and John Ely for twenty years. To the first and second articles of this statement, he says that on a certain eve of a feast day around the feast of St. Michael [29 Sept.] John came to this deponent's house and sent word to Agnes at the house of her master, Hawkyn, and Agnes immediately came. John Ely, sitting in this deponent's shop and communicating with Agnes, in the presence of this deponent, his wife Joan, and others, asked Agnes, *"Agnes, how far you?"* She responded that she was saddened because she had heard that John was going to leave her and that he intended, as they said, to take as his wife a certain widow. John took Agnes by her right hand and said to her, *"Agnes, by my feith and my trouth, I forsake all women for you and take you to my wif."* Then Agnes took John by his right hand and said to him thus, *"And by my feith and trouth, I forsake al other men in the world and take you to my husband,"* and they drank together merrily. These words were spoken around nine o'clock of that day. The deponent also says that about seven or fifteen days after this, this deponent and Joan his wife were invited by John Ely to dine with him and Agnes Whitingdon in his home. After the meal, John led Agnes, the deponent, and Joan into his chambers and showed them his beds and the clothes of his previous wife (who is now dead) and her belts. He invited Agnes to wear a certain belt on the first day of their nuptials and another belt on the second day, saying also that she could wear a blue kirtle[6] that had belonged to his first wife each day. He also showed her his bed, saying that he would never sleep in it until the marriage when she and he could sleep in it together. . . . To the fourth article, he says that the day after this contract, both John and Agnes's master, Hawkyn, came to the deponent's home. Hawkyn asked John if he wanted to marry Agnes; John replied that he would and that he had contracted with her and had made her a promise that he never wished to break and he desired Hawkyn to make an order to Master Percyvale for a piece of cloth for a wedding gown for Agnes. Hawkyn agreed to pay 6s 8d for a kirtle for Agnes, which the deponent saw and heard for himself. Another time the aforesaid John, seeing Agnes carrying clothes for laundry, asked her why she was carrying it and said in the presence of John Cok that he does not want his wife carrying clothes. To the fifth article, . . .

he says that their contract is known by public voice in the parish of St. Margaret.

John Cok, of the parish of St. Margaret Moses, has lived there since a year ago the last feast of St. Michael [29 Sept.], linen draper, literate, of free condition, fifty-eight years old, sworn etc. He has known Agnes for three years, John for half a year. Questioned about the contents of the statement, he says that on many days around the feast of St. Michael, this deponent heard John Ely, both in the home of John Roberd and his wife and in their presences, and also in the houses of this deponent and John Ely himself, saying that he wished to have Agnes as his wife and that he wished John Roberd to inquire about a wedding gown of violet for Agnes because he, John, would have a fur-trimmed gown. He also heard John saying that he did not wish Agnes to carry the laundry to the Thames and he would rather pay someone else to do the carrying than have her do it. If Agnes's master dismissed her from his service because she would not carry clothes to the Thames for washing, John would take her in and pay for her meals until the time that the marriage was celebrated between them.

13. **Robert Smyth v. Rose Langtoft** (GLRO, MS DL/C/205, fols. 166r–168r; 172v–175r; 182v)

People were willing to perjure themselves in the court in order to make or break a marriage. In this case disparity of wealth and a master's influence are at issue.

Depositions

30 September 1472

Thomas Hynkley of the parish of St. Mary Abchurch, sherman, where he has lived for a year and a half, somewhat literate, of free condition, twenty-four years old. He says that he has known Robert Smyth for seven years and Rose Langtoft for a year and a half. To the first, second, third, and fourth articles of the statement, he says that on the eve of the dedication of the church of the Blessed Mary Abchurch, occurring within five days after the last feast of St. Peter in Chains [1 Aug.], around the hour of three in the afternoon, Rose Langtoft came to this deponent's house. Soon after Robert Smyth also entered. Robert and Rose met one another in the high chamber of the house, where this deponent's wife Alice was lying sick. There before this deponent and Alice his wife and no others, Robert and Rose spoke together about a contract of marriage previously made between them. At length Rose broke out in these words, saying to Robert Smyth, "I have come here now to this place to make a change in my plans with you." Robert responded, "You cannot change things now; I want you to say here and recite here the things that we said to one another before." Then Rose relented and said, "Now I am prepared to say these things." She took him by his right hand and said to him, "I take you as my husband, and thereto I give you my faith." They unclasped their hands and immediately Robert took Rose by the hand and said to her, "And I take you, Rose, as my wife, and thereto I give you my faith," and they kissed one another. Robert Smyth gave Rose a groat,[7] which she happily received. . . . To the fifth article, he says that these things were publicly spoken about in the parish of St. Mary Abchurch. . . . To the second question, he says that for a year and a quarter before the last feast of St. Bartholomew, this deponent was Robert's co-worker and together they worked in their trade with William Repyngale, who directed them. . . . To the third question, he says that the aforesaid words were spoken and the contract made between the parties by the side of the bed in the abovesaid chamber. . . . To the fourth question, he says that at the time of the contract, Robert sat on the side of the bed and Rose at the time of the contract stood between his legs. He says that Robert was wearing a black tunic called in English *a jaket* and Rose was wearing a red tunic. He says that word of the contract was spread as far as this deponent knows by the aforesaid William Rypyngale and his wife, by James Nasshefeld, and by many others whom he does not remember at the moment, and he heard it said from others in the public street of the parish of Abchurch daily by the greater part of the parish from the time of the contract. He had come to his house to look after his wife, who as he said was lying ill at the time. . . . To the fifth question, he says that he believes that the parents of the aforesaid Rose are richer than Robert's parents.

2 October 1472

Alice Hynkeley of the parish of St. Mary Abchurch, of free condition, nineteen years old and more. She says that she has known Robert Smyth for one year and Rose Langtoft for two years. Questioned further about the contents of the statement, she agrees with the testimony of Thomas Hynkeley given above, . . . adding this, that Rose recognized before Repyngale's wife and this deponent and none others in Repyngale's house, within a month of the contract, that she, Rose, was Robert's true and lawful wife and that he was her husband.

Depositions

Responses personally made by Rose Langtoft, 2 October

To the first, second, third, and fourth charges, she says that on the day of St. James [25 July] last past, after noon and after vespers, around the hour of five, the aforesaid Robert Smyth and this deponent discussed together and talked about contracting marriage between them, near the doorway of Thomas Howden, who lives in Candlewick street. This deponent promised Robert that she wanted to take him as her husband if her parents would give their consent. And she made a similar promise to Robert Smyth many times since the feast of St. James. But any other promise, communication, or contract she has neither made nor initiated with Robert, there or anywhere.

4 November, 1472

Thomas Howdon of the parish of St. Mary Abchurch, of the city of London, tailor, literate, of free condition, about thirty-eight years old. He says that he has known Rose Langtoft for six years and more, Robert Smyth for eight or nine years, Thomas Hynkeley and Alice his wife for eight weeks. . . . To the first part of the exceptions, he says that Thomas Hynkeley and Alice Hynkeley . . . were and are much greater friends with Robert Smyth than they are with Rose Langtoft. . . . To the second part of the exceptions, he says that on the eve of the dedication of the church of St. Mary Abchurch, London, which this year occurred on the Monday immediately following the feast of Saint Peter in Chains, Rose Langtoft was his servant. As his servant he saw her continually in his house serving him and working for him on household things at his house in Candlewick Street from two o'clock in the afternoon until five o'clock, except when this deponent left the house between the hours of two and three to do some business. He came back to his house a little before three o'clock and saw Rose working inside his house. There he stayed with Rose until four o'clock and then he went to the church of St. Mary Abchurch where he heard compline; when that was finished, he returned to his house, where he saw Rose working there as before. Thus he believes in his conscience that Thomas Hynkeley and Alice his wife are perjurers, saying and affirming in their depositions that Rose was in Thomas Hynkeley's house at about three o'clock on that day and that there she contracted marriage with Robert Smyth. . . . To the third part of the exceptions, he says also that the aforesaid Thomas Hynkeley and Alice his wife were perjuring themselves by saying that Rose was wearing on that day about three o'clock a red tunic, when in fact she was wearing an old gown of murrey,[8] and throughout the whole day was dressed like that as this deponent saw. . . . To the second question, he says that between two o'clock and five o'clock Rose was sometimes in the hall and sometimes in the kitchen, most of the time in the kitchen. . . . To the third question, he says that throughout the whole day he was in his home, except as he testified above, and except in the morning between seven and eight, when he was busy outside his house with his business with Henry Lee, in the house of John Mathewe, linen draper. He says that in those times he was not continually in Rose's presence, but most of the time he was in his shop, and at three o'clock Rose was in the kitchen. He says that he can depose about Rose's wearing of the tunic of murrey because he saw her wearing the tunic the whole day, as he says. . . . To the fifth question, he says that from two o'clock until just before three, Rose was busy in the hall of the house washing clothes and from that time until five o'clock she was in the kitchen working on preparing food because of the feast the following day; sometimes she walked and sometimes she sat. The reason he was present there is because he is the head of the household. . . . To the seventh question, he says that he believes in his conscience that what they have deposed is impossible. . . . To the eighth question, he says that he does not think it would be suitable for Robert to marry Rose. . . . To the ninth question, he says that he would not be sorry, as he believes, if they did remain married.

5 November

William Taylbos, apprentice of Thomas Howden, of the parish of St. Mary Abchurch, with whom he has lived for five years and more, literate, of free condition, nineteen years old. He says he has known Rose Langtoft for seven years, Robert Smyth for eight, Thomas Hynkeley for the last six weeks, and Alice his wife for two weeks. . . . To the first part of the exceptions, he agrees with the testimony of Thomas Howden given above. To the second part of the exceptions, he says that from the hour of noon on that day to five o'clock, Rose stayed for the entire time inside the house of Thomas Howden, his master, at no time leaving the house. He knows this because he sat in the shop of that house openly, next to the street, for that whole time, where he could have seen Rose leaving the house if she were so disposed and returning, but he did not see her do this. Thus he believes that the aforesaid Thomas Hynkeley and Alice, his wife, are perjurers for saying in their depositions that Rose contracted marriage with Robert Smyth in Thomas Hynkeley's house about the hour of three on that day, for it is impossible for Rose to be at one and the same time in the houses of Thomas Hynkeley and Thomas Howden. . . . To the second question, he says for that entire time he was in the shop and in the house. . . . To the third question, he says that between the hours of two and three after noon he left the shop and came into the hall of the house, where he saw Rose washing clothes, and immediately after he returned to the shop, where he remained, as he deposed before. Otherwise he was not in the presence of Rose between the hours of twelve and five. . . . To the fifth question, he says that Rose had told him that after she had washed the clothes she wanted to prepare the food for the next day. . . . To the eighth question, he says that it is certainly suitable for Robert to have Rose in marriage just as it is suitable for her to have him as her husband. To the ninth question, he would not be sorry to see them joined together in marriage.

16 January 1473

Rose Langtoft appeared before the lord Official, . . . and admitted and recognized in the presence of Robert Smyth that she had contracted marriage with him in this form, Robert saying first, "I, Robert, accept you, Rose, as my wife, and thereto I give you my faith," and Rose responding to him, "And I, Rose, take you, Robert, as my husband, and thereto I give you my faith." They then kissed one another. She says that the contract was made on the Saturday after the feast of St. Katherine [25 Nov.], in the home of William Portlouth, in the parish of St. Benet Gracechurch. Moreover, Rose admitted that a contract was made between Robert and Rose in the home of Thomas Hynkeley as Thomas Hynkeley and Alice his wife deposed above, and this was in their house on the day Thomas and Alice deposed, as she says under oath.

False Testimony

14. Joan Perot v. John Mendham and Elizabeth Seyve
(GLRO, MS DL/C/205, fols. 58v–59v)

Others perjured themselves in order to save a loved one's reputation. This deposition also reveals interesting attitudes towards sin and culpability.

28 March 1470

Thomas Hervy, gentleman, of Rickinghall [Suffolk], diocese of Norwich, literate, of free condition, thirty-four years old. He says that he has known Joan Perot from the feast of the purification of the Blessed Virgin [2 Feb.] last, and John Mendham for sixteen years and Elizabeth Seyve for about nine years. . . . To the first part of the exceptions, he says that he knows only that Henry Exnynge, the brother of William Exnynge, married Elizabeth Seyve's grandmother. In Henry's house Elizabeth was well loved, educated, and fed, from her childhood, as their daughter. Thus she was publicly and commonly said to be William Exnynge's affine [relative by marriage] at Newmarket and other neighboring places, as far this deponent knew. . . . To the second part of the exceptions, he says that on Monday or Tuesday or Wednesday before Quinquagesima Sunday [26–28 Feb.] (he cannot recall which of the three days it was) this deponent was in the upper hall of John Mendham's house at the sign of the Bells at Aldgate, London, around the hour of six in the morning. William Exnynge entered and spoke to John Mendham, asking him where his sister Elizabeth was, and John Mendham replied that she had left him and was in Staining Lane at St. Martin's. Then this deponent asked William what his name was, and he responded that his name was William Exnynge of Ware [Hertfordshire]. This deponent asked William then what sort of conscience he had, who had deposed in the matrimonial cause between Elizabeth and John Mendham and had made them joined together in marriage against law and conscience, causing them to live together in adultery by his false deposition. William asked this deponent who told him such things, and he answered that it was John Mendham there present and Elizabeth Seyve. Then William, in the presence of this deponent, John Mendham, John Metcalf, and Thomas Marys, swore at John Mendham and Elizabeth, because by their false information and instruction, he had deposed and offered false testimony for them, and for this false witness he had had and would have seven years of penance[9] enjoined on him by his curate. He added moreover that he gave this false testimony for love of Elizabeth, his affine, and to save her reputation, and that he had had from John Mendham for his labor and for his expenses only a hat, in English *a Bonet*. He said that before his deposition was made, John Mendham and Elizabeth had instructed him that even if he had not heard any matrimonial words spoken between them, he should not worry about deposing in the case, because they would take all the danger on their own souls and answer before God for it.

Multiple Contracts and Bigamy

15. **Robert Grene v. Maude Knyff** and **Thomas Torald v. Maude Knyff** (GLRO, MS DL/C/205, fols. 60v–68r)

Some people made several contracts within a short period and the court's job was to determine which contract came first. This case involves an apparently wealthy widow with two eager suitors.

Depositions

13 July 1470

Arnold Snarynge, of the parish of Hackford [Norfolk], Norwich diocese, gentleman, where he has lived for twelve years and is the lord of the manor, literate, of free condition, about forty years of age, as he says. He has known Robert Grene for about a year and Maude Knyff, widow of the parish of St. Sepulchre, for five years. . . . To the first and second articles of the statement, he says that on Wednesday a week ago [4 July], before noon, Robert Grene came to him in the public road leading to the town of Islington, across from the house of St. John of Jerusalem in England,[10] and told him that he had contracted marriage with Maude. Robert Grene asked Arnold if he would come that afternoon to Maude's house, situated on the west part of the church of St. Sepulchre, to hear what would be said between them. In the afternoon, between the hours of six and seven, this deponent came to Maude's house, together with John Pomeys. This deponent and John Pomeys, and no others, stood in the street at the stall of Maude's house and peered in through the window called *le latys*. In a certain lower parlor there, they saw first Robert Grene, wearing a gown of murrey, and Maude, wearing a black tunic or kirtle with an apron, standing together. Maude was embracing Robert around the neck with her right arm and Robert was holding Maude's right hand in his right hand. There and then, before any communication between them, Robert, with his left hand, took from Maude's left hand a gold ring. When that was done, Maude asked Robert to guard that ring well, out of love for her, because she would not want that ring to be lost, out of love for her deceased husband. She said to Robert, their hands still joined together, *"Robert I shall never have husband but you and þerto Y plyght the my trouth a fore god."* Then

68

Robert said, their hands still joined, *"Gra mercy, maistres Mawlt, I shall never have other wyf but you and perto Y plyght you my trouth a fore god."* They then kissed one another, as this deponent testifies from his own sight and hearing, as he would swear before the Highest Judge in the Day of Judgment. He says also that neither before that Wednesday nor after did he ever hear Robert and Maude communicating about these matters. . . . To the second question, he says that on that day this deponent wore the gown of tawny that he is wearing right now and his fellow witness was wearing a gown of russet,[11] as he believes.

Responses personally made by Maude Knyff, 19 July, 1470

She denies the first, second, third, and fourth charges made against her, except that she says that on a certain day, exactly when she does not recall, fifteen days or more ago, this deponent and Robert Grene were sitting together in the shop at her house, in the lower parlor situated near the street, in the street called Snow Hill in the parish of St. Sepulchre without Newgate. They were communicating together about certain matters, but what they talked about she cannot remember at present. While they were talking, Robert took this deponent by the left hand and took a gold ring with a blue-colored stone from one of her fingers, that is from her little finger, against her will. Another time within the last three weeks, this deponent was in the garden in her house at Islington. She had a kerchief tied around a wound, but it fell onto the ground, and Robert Grene immediately picked it up and kept it again against the will of this deponent, and he keeps it still to this day.

Depositions

21 July 1470

Joan Bristall, wife of Richard Bristall of the parish of St. Sepulchre, of free condition, forty years old. She says that she has known Thomas Torald from a week ago Tuesday, and Maude Knyff for twelve years. To the first and second parts of the statement, she says that a week ago Tuesday, Richard Bristall, the husband of this deponent, ordered her to go to the house of Maude Knyff and there hear how Maude was affianced to a certain man. Immediately at the order of her husband she went to Maude's house between the hours of three and four in the afternoon, and there in the upper hall she found Thomas Torald and Maude sitting together at the end of the high table of the house. Immediately Maude said to this deponent, "Behold, here sits my husband." Then Thomas asserted publicly then and there that Maude was his wife, and said to this deponent, "For the greater and more evident notice of this matter, know that this Maude is my wife." He took her by the hand and said to her, "I, Thomas, take you, Maude, as my wife, as long as we shall live, and thereto I give you my faith," and they unclasped their hands. Then Maude took him by the hand and said to him in this form in English, *"So am Y as longe as my lyf lastyth, and þerto Y plyght you my trouth."* . . . Questioned further about who was present there and listening to the aforesaid, she said that the couple themselves, this deponent, Robert Longe, Agnes his wife, John Preston, and as she believes, Richard Bristall, the deponent's husband, and none others as she recalls at present, except the servants of the house, and whether the servants heard the words spoken or not she does not know. After that this deponent left the house but then immediately came back, entering again into the hall, and there were present this deponent, James Mamford, John Davy, and Audrey Quynson, and none others, as she believes. Then Thomas Torald asserted publicly again, "Behold, Maude is my wife," and she said, "And you are my husband; behold the sign," holding up the gold ring on the index finger of her right hand. Then Thomas took her by the hand and said to her, "I, Thomas, take you, Maude, as my wife, and thereto I give you my faith," and they unclasped their hands, and she took him by the hand and said to him, "And I, Maude, take you Thomas as my husband and thereto I give you my faith.". . . . To the third question, she says that at the time of the contract the two contracting parties were sitting at the end of the table. To the fourth question, she says that she has greater affection for Thomas Torald and Maude than for Robert Grene, if law and justice permit it, otherwise not. She says that she doesn't care who wins the case as long as justice is done. To the fifth question, she says that in the parish of St. Sepulchre it is publicly said by many parishioners that certain gentlemen friends of Robert publicly said that Robert contracted marriage with Maude, and that he had known her carnally. . . . To the sixth question, she says that before her examination, this deponent said this of Robert Grene: *"He is a boy and a knave. I truste to god he shall have a fall in his matier and he schall be hanged. Fye on him, fals theff."* To the seventh question, she says that once in the presence of this deponent, her husband, Maude, Audrey Quynson, Agnes Longe, and others whom she does not remember now, Robert rode on a horse to Holloway, and from there to Finchley, and another time she saw him in Maude's house, long before the present suit.

16. Richard Smalwode v. Agnes Twytynge and Robert Hilton and Robert Tryse v. Agnes Twetynge, Richard Smalwode, and Robert Hilton (GLRO, MS DL/C/205, fols. 108v–110v, 115r–115v, 124r–124v)

While a case was being heard before an ecclesiastical court, the couple was often officially prohibited from making another contract of marriage with another party. In this case, a man eager to marry a woman with a case before the court pulls strings so that he can solemnize a marriage with her in a church. (Note that this ceremony, even though it is held in a church, is called clandestine, because it was illicitly procured.) Legally it was the prior contract, if properly made, that was valid, regardless of where it took place.

Responses personally made by Robert Hilton, 29 May 1471

To the first question, he says that he heard that Richard Smalwode was prosecuting Agnes Twytynge before the Official and the Consistory of London in a certain matrimonial cause. . . . To the second question, he says that he heard Agnes Twytynge saying to him that Master John Lord, her proctor, inhibited Agnes from solemnizing any marriage by the order of the Lord Official of the Consistory of London and, pending the suit between her and Richard Smalwode, she is not to marry anyone else. To the third question, he says that after he had notice of the inhibition and the intimation abovesaid, this deponent and Agnes procured the solemnization of marriage between them in the church of Paddington. He says that the vicar of this church, whose name he cannot specify, celebrated marriage between them on the Sunday before the feast of the Ascension of the Lord

[19 May], between the hours of ten and eleven in the morning. He says that a certain man named Cornwell, tailor, and his wife, Thomas Roger and his wife of the parish of St. Clement without Temple Bar, Thomas Pernell, Richard Bele, John Mantell, John Grene, John Maynard, Thomas Richardson, a certain man named John living next to Lyon's Alley who is a hosier, and William Pepyr, butcher of the parish of St. Nicholas in the Shambles, London, were present at that solemnization. He says that Thomas Parnell and Cornwell gave him advice about how to solemnize the marriage and the vicar received for his labor forty pence besides the offerings made at the mass. He says moreover that at the second reading of the banns between this deponent and Agnes, Richard Smalwode shouted out against them, both in the church of St. Clement and in the church of St. Nicholas in the Shambles, London.

29 May 1471

John Cornwell of the parish of St. Clement's without Temple Bar, London, tailor, where he has lived for forty years and more, illiterate, of free condition, about sixty years of age. He says that he has known Robert Hilton for almost a year and Agnes Twytynge for seven years. To the first and second articles of the statement, he says that on the last feast of SS. Philip and James [1 May], between the hours of about four and five in the afternoon, he was present in Agnes Twytynge's house, in a parlor together with Richard Weston, Thomas Swalowe, and Agnes Gubbe, when Robert Hilton, after many discussions between him and Agnes Twytynge, burst out in these words, speaking to Agnes in this way, "Agnes, can you find it in your heart to have me as your husband?" Agnes immediately replied, "I can find it in my heart to have you as my husband, before all the other men in the world." Then Agnes, holding him by the hand, said to him, "Can you find it in your heart to have me as your wife?" Robert immediately answered, "I can find it in my heart to have you as my wife, and thereto I give you my faith." Immediately they both kissed one another, which this deponent testifies from his own sight and hearing. . . . To the first question, he says that Robert Hilton asked him many times if he would work towards a contract of marriage between him and Agnes, and so he says that he was a mediator and worked on Agnes, giving advice so that Robert could contract marriage with her. To the second question, he says that he was present at the clandestine solemnization performed by the vicar of Paddington between Robert and Agnes on the Sunday before the feast of the Ascension last, in the parish church of Paddington. He says that he put his labors and mediations towards the Archdeacon of Westminster, so that he would give them a licence to solemnize the marriage between Robert and Alice on the day and place mentioned, and by archidiaconal licence this marriage was obtained. To the third question, he says that he holds Robert and Agnes in greater affection than Richard Smalwode. He says that he wants Robert Hilton to win this case more than Richard Smalwode, because Robert Hilton has more right to Agnes than Richard Smalwode. . . . To the fifth question . . . he says that he heard it said that on the feast of the Finding of the Holy Cross [3 May] last past, in the afternoon, Richard Smalwode and Agnes contracted marriage between them in the tavern at the sign of the King's Head in Fleet Street, and this contract made between them was common knowledge in the parish of St. Clement.

Depositions

20 June 1471

John Fox of the parish of St. Clement's without Temple Bar, tailor, literate, of free condition, forty-six years old. He says that he has known Richard Smalwode for thirty years and Agnes Twytynge for five years. To the first and second articles of the statement, he says that on the feast of the Finding of the Holy Cross [3 May] last past, between the hours of one and two in the afternoon, Richard Smalwode entered this deponent's house. A little while after his entrance, Agnes Twytynge also entered into the house. Richard and Agnes, who were there with this deponent and Thomas Byllysby, sat at the table in a certain hall in this house, drinking and talking together. Among other things that they talked about, Richard and Agnes discussed contracting marriage between them. During this conversation, this deponent informed Richard how to contract marriage with Agnes, reciting these words, "I, Richard, take you, Agnes, as my wife, and thereto I give you my faith." After this recitation and instruction, Richard Smalwode spoke similar words to Agnes, thus: "I, Richard, take you, Agnes as my wife, and thereto I give you my faith."

18 December 1471

Thomas Swalowe of the parish of St. Clement's without Temple Bar, London, illiterate, of free condition, twenty years old. He says that he has known Robert Tryse since last Lent, Agnes Twetynge for eight years, Robert Hilton for half a year, and Richard Smalwode for ten years. Questioned further, he says that on a certain feast day around the last feast of the Annunciation of the Blessed Virgin [25 March], this deponent saw and heard Robert Tryse and Agnes communicating together concerning contracting marriage between them, inside Agnes Twytynge's house situated in the parish of St. Clement's aforesaid. He saw when Robert Tryse took Agnes Twetynge by her right hand and said to her, "I here give you my faith that I will take you as my wife." Then Agnes said to Robert Tryse, "You are foolish to give me your faith, because you have my faith." Then and at other times in the presence of this deponent Agnes did not speak other words sounding of marriage.

17. Henry Brown alias Lymyngton v. Margaret Brown alias Lymyngton and Richard Bishop (GLRO, MS DL/C/205, fols. 102r–104r)

As marriages could not be dissolved if they had been properly made, many couples practiced self-divorce. Either one partner deserted the other or they mutually agreed to separate. Legally they could not marry again, but many tried. Even after the lapse of many years, however, the original spouse sometimes wanted to revive the previous marriage and its validity could not be denied.

28 March 1471

John Randolf, butcher of the parish of St. Michael Queenhithe, London, illiterate, of free condition, forty-eight years old. He says that he has known Henry Brown for sixteen years, Margaret Brown alias Lymyngton from the time of the marriage made between Henry Brown and Margaret, and Richard Bysshopp for the last two weeks. Asked whether he knows of any marriage contract made or celebrated between Henry Brown and Margaret, he says that eleven or twelve years ago, he was present in the church of St. Mary le Bow, London, on a certain day which he cannot precisely recall, when and where a certain priest of the church, whose name he does not know, solemnized marriage between Henry Brown and Margaret Brown. During the solemnization, this deponent heard when Henry Brown said to Margaret, following the instructions of the priest, "I, Henry, take you, Margaret, as my wife, and thereto I give you my faith." Similarly he heard when Margaret said to Henry, following the instruction of the priest, "I, Margaret, take you, Henry, as my husband, and thereto I give you my faith." He says that on the same day, after the solemnization of marriage, this deponent offered with them in the nuptial mass. He says moreover that Henry and Margaret, after the solemnization of marriage, as this deponent knows certainly from his own sight and knowledge, lived together for a year as man and wife in the parish of St. Michael Queenhithe. He says also that in the parishes of St. Mary le Bow and St. Michael the rumor was that they had contracted marriage and solemnized it as above.

William Orton of the parish of St. Martin the Vintry, London, barber, literate, of free condition, thirty-two years old. He says that he has known Henry Brown for about three weeks and Margaret Brown alias Lymyngton for two years and Richard Bysshopp for fourteen years. Questioned further, he says that on a certain Monday within the two weeks before the last feast of Pentecost [late May 1470], he was present in the church of St. Martin the Vintry, London, where and when Master Robert Kyrkeman, rector then and now of the church, solemnized marriage around the hour of nine between Richard Bysshop and Margaret Brown alias Lymyngton. . . . He says moreover that Richard and Margaret have cohabited since that solemnization in the parish of St. Martin as man and wife, from his own sight and knowledge. He says also that there is public voice and fame of the marriage about which he has deposed in the parish of St. Martin.

Henry Brown, sworn under oath, says that about eleven years ago in the church [of St. Mary] le Bow marriage was solemnized between this deponent and Margaret by the parish chaplain of the church, whose name he does not know. In that solemnization, the chaplain instructed him what to say in the solemnization, and following the instructions he said as follows: "I, Henry, take you, Margaret, as my wife, and thereto I give you my faith." Similarly Margaret said to this deponent following the instruction of the chaplain, "I, Margaret, take you, Henry, as my husband, and thereto I give you my faith." He says that after this solemnization, Henry and Margaret lived together as man and wife in the town of Kingston-on-Thames for more than a year and a half. In a similar manner, Margaret, sworn and examined, said the same, and thus the case is finished by agreement.

Divorce: Coercion or Force and Fear

18. **Ann Munden v. Richard Bulle** and **Thomas Lak v. Ann Munden** (GL, MS 9065, fols. 15r, 17r–17v)

A divorce a vinculo *was the equivalent of an annulment: the marriage never actually existed. Usually these were granted on the grounds of a prior contract, as in some of the cases above. But in this case Ann Munden sought a divorce a vinculo from Richard Bulle both because she alleged a prior contract and because she contended that she had been coerced in her marriage to him. As it was*

*consent which made the marriage, a contract which
was not voluntarily made was invalid. Generally,
however, the courts looked upon subsequent cohab-
itation as mitigating any coercion.*

Responses of Ann Munden, 28 November [1486?]

To the first and second charges, . . . she says that on the
eve of Epiphany [6 Jan.] four years ago she and Thomas Lak
contracted marriage in the home of William Byrd of Ware
[Hertfordshire], about the hour of three or four in the afternoon, in the presence of William Byrd, John Braghing, and
Richard Smyth. They said to each other, *"I, Thomas, take
the, Anny, to my wife,"* and *"I take the to my husband."* Matrimonial banns were read between them three times in the
church of Ware, in the presence of Richard Bulle. . . . To the
fourth charge, this deponent says that on the Wednesday after
the feast of the Purification of the Blessed Mary [2 Feb.] four
years ago she was compelled to be married to Richard Bulle
in the chapel of the Holy Trinity near Hertford. Around thir-
teen days before this said marriage, Richard Bulle and Carl
Newell violently apprehended her and held her in their custo-
dy, against her will, in Carl's house and in other places until
the day of the aforesaid wedding. Afterwards, she and Richard Bulle cohabited as man and wife in this deponent's house
in the parish of Ware for about two years.

4 May [1487?]

William Byrd of Ware, in the diocese of London, where
he has lived for thirty years, illiterate, of free condition,
fifty-six years old. He has known Thomas Lak for sixteen
years and Ann Munden for forty years. To the first and second articles, he says that on the eve of the feast of the Epi-

phany [6 Jan.] five years ago, this deponent was present in
his own house in Ware, in a certain lower parlor, together
with Thomas Lak, Ann Munden, Richard Smyth, and M.
Brawghing. After discussion between them about contracting
marriage, Thomas took Ann by the right hand and said to
her thus, *"Anne, and [if] ye be as cler a woman as I am a
man, I take you to my wif, and therto I pliȝt you my trouth."*
Anne responded to him, *"If ye be as cler a man as I am a
woman, I take you to my husbond and therto I pliȝt you my
trouth."* They withdrew their hands and kissed each other.
Afterwards, matrimonial banns were read three times in the
church of Ware. On the third reading, a certain Richard
Bulle cried out against the reading of such a bann, as the
deponent saw and heard. . . . To the fourth article, he says
that four or five days before the feast of the Purification [2
Feb.] five years ago, the deponent was in the chapel of the
Holy Trinity near the village of Hertford, where a White
Friar of the order of the Redemption of Captives[12] solemnized matrimony between Richard Bulle and Ann, no banns
being read between them beforehand in the parish church as
far as this deponent knew or heard. There were present there
together with the deponent William Brend, Thomas Fox, a
certain man named Spynke, and another named Turtyll. The
deponent was present there at the solemnization of marriage
because of fear of Richard Bulle's master, who was at that
time bailiff of Ware. After the solemnization of marriage,
Richard and Ann cohabited in the parish of Ware as man and
wife for about two years.

Richard Smyth of Ware, where he has lived for fifteen
years, illiterate, of free condition, forty-six years old. He has
known Thomas Lak for fifteen years, and Ann Munden for

the same period. To the first, second, and third articles he says that he agrees with the testimony of his fellow witness, William Byrd. To the fourth article, he says that on a certain day after the contract, Ann, in the home of the deponent, told the deponent that a certain Richard Bulle, whom she said she had never seen before, wanted to marry her and that, because of fear of death, she did not dare resist him. She said that Richard, with his accomplices, abducted her from the town of Ware and had marriage solemnized between himself and Ann in a certain chapel of the Holy Trinity near Hertford, as this deponent had heard said, banns not being read between them. The deponent also said that after the solemnization of the marriage, Richard and Ann cohabited in the parish as man and wife for about two years.

19. Agnes Wellys v. William Rote (GLRO, MS DL/C/205, fols. 265v–266v)

In this medieval equivalent of a "shotgun wedding," William Rote claims that his contract with Agnes Wellys was made under compulsion and thus is not valid. The case presents interesting evidence about the importance of female chastity and the power of public embarrassment.

Responses of William Rote, 10 March 1475

. . . To the second charge, he said that on the eve of the Assumption of the Blessed Virgin, he was present in the house of John Wellys about the hour of two in the afternoon. He had come with a jug of wine to drink with John Wellys, the head of that household. But when he got there John Wellys said to him: "You have violated Agnes, my daughter, and have known her carnally. You will contract marriage with her if I have to force you and you will be sorry." This deponent responded that he had never known Agnes carnally and so he didn't want to contract marriage with her. Then John Wellys, in the presence of Agnes Wellys and Thomas Barbour and his wife, took out a dagger as if he meant to stab this deponent. He appeared to be very angry and he was lifting his arm to stab this deponent when Thomas Barbour stepped between them and Wellys pulled back. This deponent took the opportunity to flee and ran out of the house onto the public street. Both Agnes's mother and Agnes herself ran after him, shouting, *"Holde the thef."* They caught him and brought him back to the house, where John Wellys was waiting, still very angry. Wellys said that unless this deponent would contract marriage with his daughter Agnes, he or someone else in his name would give this deponent a sign that he would take with him to his grave. Wellys also said that he would bring this deponent before the mayor and alderman where he would be confounded by such embarrassment that the shame would compel him to contract marriage with Agnes. So, as much from fear of his body and from shame at appearing before the mayor and aldermen, this deponent contracted marriage there with Agnes.

Divorce: Cruelty

20. **Eleanor Brownynge v. Alexander Brownynge** (GLRO, MS DL/C/205, fols. 203v–204r)

A divorce a mensa et thoro, *or a legal separation, could be sought on a number of grounds, including adultery and heresy. All but one of the few divorce cases in the deposition books were sought, howev-*

er, on the grounds of cruelty. The criteria were stringent; this witness and the others in the case emphasized the danger to Eleanor Brownynge's life if she were to remain married to her husband.

William Saunder of the parish of St. Benet Fink, London, sherman, of free condition, forty years old and more. He says that he has known Alexander Brownynge for seven years and Eleanor Brownynge for eight years. Questioned further, he says that on a day in summer seven years ago, this deponent, coming with a repaired gown to the home of a man named Burgoyn situated in the hospital of St. Bartholomew, saw Alexander with a naked dagger in his hand chasing after Eleanor, who was running in her tunic with her head uncovered and her hair streaming behind her. Because of fear, Eleanor ran to the house of the man named Burgoyn, where Eleanor's sister was. Eleanor's sister took her into the house and closed the door. Alexander, seeing this, shouted in a loud voice, swearing that he wanted to kill Eleanor the next time he saw her unless those in the house gave her up to him. When they would not do this, Alexander left. This deponent says in his conscience that Eleanor would have been killed or at least mutilated if she had not escaped into the house. He says moreover that within the last five years on a certain day, exactly when he does not recall, Alexander entered the tavern at the sign of the Sun on Lombard Street, London, where, in the presence of this deponent, he held a naked dagger in his hand, and threatened Eleanor with it. On account of his threat, Eleanor jumped at least the distance of four men long, which this deponent saw with his own eyes.

Depositions

Fornication

21. **Joan Chylde v. Thomas Rote** (GLRO, MS DL/C/205, fols. 191r–193r)

> *This case shows the interest of local secular courts in the sexual lives of Londoners. The ward moot was a meeting of twelve men appointed by the alderman of a ward to investigate crimes in the ward, among which they included fornication and adultery. (There were twenty-five wards in London; this ward was Broad Street.) This case came to the Consistory Court because Thomas Rote failed to keep the contract of marriage he had allegedly made before the ward moot.*

14 June 1473

William White of the parish of St. Margaret Lothbury, founder, literate, of free condition, thirty-six years old, as he says, sworn as a witness, etc. He says that he has known Joan Chylde and Thomas Rote from a year ago last Christmas. To the first, second, and third parts of this statement, he says that on a certain feast day between Christmas and the Purification of the Virgin Mary [2 Feb.] a year ago, as he believes, which day he cannot specify, around three o'clock in the afternoon, this deponent came, together with eleven other men from the neighborhood, just outside the west door of the church of the Austin friars of the city of London, to have a meeting of the Twelve, vulgarly called the inquest of the ward moot. In the presence of the ward moot, Thomas Rote personally appeared, having been previously detected to the Twelve concerning fornication committed by him and Joan Chylde. One of the Twelve, whose name he cannot recall at this moment, asked Thomas why he kept company in this way with Joan Chylde, and Thomas, in front of the Twelve and of Joan Chylde who was also there similarly detected to the Twelve, answered that he kept company with Joan in this way because he intended to make her a good woman, as he said. He said moreover that he wished to have her as his wife. Joan Chylde, in the presence of this deponent and the other men, responded right away that she also wished to have Thomas as her husband. Thomas said first to the Twelve and to Joan, "I will have Joan as my wife"; Joan then said to the Twelve and to Thomas, "And I will have Thomas as my husband." Before this deponent and the Twelve, they both kissed one another, which this deponent testifies from his own sight and hearing. Otherwise he has nothing else to depose concerning these parts [of the statement], except that Joan and Thomas were dismissed from the ward moot because of the words they had spoken before the Twelve, and they were not presented to the Alderman of the Ward, as he says. . . .

Responses personally made by Thomas Rote on the same day

To the second charge, he says that he said these words before the aforesaid Twelve and in the presence of Joan at that time and place: that if Joan was well governed, he would want to do more for her than for any other woman in the world. He does not recall saying any other words regarding marriage, but he says that he kissed her in the presence of the Twelve. . . . To the fourth charge, he says that he believes that the common rumor in the parish of St. Benet Gracechurch since that day has been that this deponent and Joan contracted marriage together.

Depositions

22. Joan Sebar v. Joan Rokker (GL, MS 9065, fols. 267r–267v)

In this defamation case, the witnesses appearing on behalf of Joan Sebar claim that Joan Rokker's allegations that Joan Sebar fornicated in a doorway gravely harm Sebar's chances of marrying.

19 January 1497

Henry Patenson of the parish of St. Mary Woolchurch, London, where he has lived for seven years, illiterate, of free condition, about fifty years old. . . . He says that after vespers on the Sunday immediately after the last feast of the blessed Mary, this deponent was crossing from his parish church to his own house when he heard Joan Rokker in the public street near the house of Richard Goloser scolding Joan Sebar, who was standing in Goloser's doorway and entrance. In a malicious and angry spirit, as it appeared to this deponent, she said to Joan Sebar, *"Thou strong hoor and strong harlot,"* and threw a piece of bread at her head. A certain Elizabeth, another servant of Richard Goloser, threw the bread back at Joan Rokker's head. Joan Rokker picked it up again and, holding it up, said to Joan Sebar, *"Go home thou strong hor and bid thi dame ordeyne the clowtis[13]; and [if] ever I had child in my belly thou hast one. Her wer thou dight,[14] and her ley thi leggis and her thi <fete>,"* pointing at the doorway into the house next to Richard Goloser's. . . . To the sixth article, he says that because of the speaking of these defamatory words, the status and good fame of Joan Sebar was greatly wounded. . . . He believes in his conscience that Joan Sebar, who is a young woman and suitable for a husband, is so wounded from the speaking of these words that she will never or only with great difficulty overcome the wounding of her fame.

Depositions

William Gerard of the parish of St. Mary Woolchurch, city of London, where he has lived for a year and more, illiterate, of free condition, forty years old and more. He says that he has known Joan Sebar for about a year and Joan Rokker from about the last feast of All Saints. . . . He agrees with Henry Patenson's testimony. . . . He says that if this deponent were single and free to contract marriage, he would give her little faith or favor and would more quickly refuse to marry her because of the imposition of this crime on her.

Adultery

23. **William Stevenes v. John Palmer** (GLRO, MS DL/C/205, fols. 142r–143r)

In this case, William Stevenes sues John Palmer for defamation. Palmer alleges that he witnessed Stevenes committing adultery and, presumably because he feels it was his moral duty, he has informed a number of ecclesiastical and civic officials about it.

Responses personally made by John Palmer, 2 March 1472

To the fifth and sixth charges, he says that on the fifteenth day of the month of August last past, he was present in the home of a certain man named Horne Tyler, situated within the parish of St. John Walbrook, London, where and when, between the hours of four and five in the afternoon, he entered alone into the house. There he saw the said William Stevenes and Juliana Saunder lying on a bed in a certain upper chamber of the house, having sexual intercourse. As this deponent was standing on the stairway leading up and into the said room, he saw Juliana lying on the bed and she spoke to him at the time of the abovesaid intercourse, saying, "Who's there—Palmer?" This deponent immediately responded, "I'm almost there." After he said these words, William Stevenes and Juliana separated, and Juliana came down from the room and asked him to keep what he had seen there secret and not to reveal to anyone what he had seen. If he would do this, Juliana promised him a pair of hose. He says moreover that since the fifteenth of August, this deponent has told Sir Walter, at that time parish chaplain of the church of St. John in Walbrook, the parish priest of the church of St. Mary at Hill, the twelve of the ward moot, the holy water clerk of the church of St. John Walbrook, and others, that William Stevenes and Juliana committed adultery at the place and time abovementioned, as he says. To the seventh and eighth charges, he says that since the feast of Christmas last, on a certain day (he cannot be more specific), this deponent had written a document, affixed to a deed, which contains the truth, which he handed over to Master William Alyard, and the tenor of it was read aloud to him at the time of his examination. He admitted then that the contents of it are true, as this deponent will answer before God on the Day of Judgment, as he says.

Notes

1. William Langland, *Piers Plowman: An Alliterative Verse Translation*, trans. E. Talbot Donaldson, ed. Elizabeth D. Kirk and Judith H. Anderson (New York: W.W. Norton, 1990), B Text, Passus ix, lines 116–19.

2. The title "Sir" was used for priests as well as knights.

3. The MS is unclear; it could be Waltham (Essex).

4. A coin worth 3s 4d.

5. A mark was worth two-thirds of a pound (i.e., 13s 4d).

6. A decorative overgown worn by women.

7. A coin worth 4d.

8. Reddish-purple colored cloth, the color of mulberries.

9. The standard ecclesiastical penance for perjury.

10. The Priory of St. John in Clerkenwell of the Hospitallers of St. John, a military order.

11. Tawny is yellowish-brown cloth and Russet is either gray or reddish-brown.

12. Either a Carmelite or perhaps a member of an obscure mendicant order, the Mercederians.

13. I.e., make swaddling clothes.

14. 'Dight' in this case is probably a verb meaning to fornicate.